CONTENTS

NOTE

The documentary material in this reader is divided into sections which focus on particular aspects of the history of the Labour Party 1881 to 1951. There is a brief introduction to historiography, debates and sources for the study of the history of the Labour Party. Thereafter, each chapter is prefaced by a commentary which provides a background to the extracts, with numbers in brackets referring to the documents which follow.

ABBREVIATIONS

ILP: Independent Labour Party
LRC: Labour Representation Committee
NAC: National Administrative Council (of the ILP)
NATO: North Atlantic Treaty Organisation
NEC: National Executive Committee (of the Labour Party)
NHS: National Health Service
PRO: Public Record Office
PLP: Parliamentary Labour Party
WEC: War Emergency Committee

INTRODUCTION: THE LABOUR PARTY 1881–1951: ISSUES INTERPRETATIONS AND SOURCES

The emergence of the Labour Party and its development over almost ninety years are events of more than usual significance for our time. The early years of the twentieth century saw the Labour Party replacing the Liberal Party as the progressive force in British politics, raising it alongside the Conservative Party as one of the two major parties in British parliamentary politics. Whilst politicians and historians have speculated about the future of the Labour Party since the early 1950s, there were few doubts about the growing prospects of Labour in the first half of the twentieth century. The collapse of the second Labour government in August 1931 and the humiliating defeat of the Labour Party in the October 1931 General Election were considered to be temporary setbacks, produced by Ramsay Mac-Donald's callous and cowardly betrayal of the Labour movement and reflected in a popular catch in Labour circles which suggested that MacDonald, and his fellow conspirators, should be hung 'from a sour apple tree' for 'That's the place where traitors ought to be'.[1] Throughout the 1930s the Party recovered ground quickly and reached its apotheosis in the Attlee governments of 1945 and 1951. Indeed, from its early beginnings, in the socialist groups of the 1880s and 1890s, through to the defeat of Attlee's administration in 1951, there was an almost Whiggish belief amongst many Labour supporters that the Party would grow inexorably and that the 'Cause' of socialism was about to be realised. Doubts about Labour's future were generally short-lived.

This Reader is concerned with the years of Labour expansion up to 1951, not with the period of doubt and soul-searching which, with the exception of the mid 1960s, has dogged the Party's existence ever since. It deals with the factors which have most affected the emergence of the Labour Party and the crucial events which have shaped the contours of its history up to 1951 – most notably Liberal Radicalism, the trade union movement, the formation of the Labour Representation Committee in 1900, the collapse of the second Labour government in 1931, and the creation of the welfare state during the Attlee years.

From its early days, the Labour Party has been influenced by the competing demands about its role, purpose and ideology. Ramsay MacDonald, despite moves to win trade-union support through the formation of the LRC in 1900, believed in a party which attracted all the social classes – a conception which was also held by later Labour leaders and the current leadership. But between MacDonald and Kinnock lies an age when the Labour Party became, through the agency of the trade union movement, the party of the working class. And, in many respects, socialism to trade unionism came to mean little more than nationalization.

As the history of the Labour Party has evolved it has produced several debates which have fascinated historians. Currently, there are five major debates raging over the history of the Labour Party before 1951. The first, and the most controversial, has revolved around the question, why did the Party emerge and, as a subsiduary, why did the Liberal Party decline? Those who have debated the fortunes of the Liberal and Labour parties have sought a turnover point. Did the Labour Party emerge before the First World War or did it emerge as a result of the Asquith v Lloyd George split in 1916, creating a political lacuna which Labour filled. On the whole, those on the Left have tended to accept that the Labour Party was well and truly on course for political success by the beginning of the First World War, due to the experience of class politics and the fact that the Liberals were no longer able to respond to the demands of the working class. As George Dangerfield wrote in *The Strange Death of Liberal England*, more than fifty years ago, the 'death knell of Liberalism was ringing' well before 1914 and that after the 1906 General Election the Liberal Party was no longer the left in British parliamentary politics.[2] Trevor Wilson, on the other hand, writing in *The Downfall of the Liberal Party 1914–1935*, has suggested that it was 'the rampant omnibus of war', not class politics, which initiated the process of disintegration within the Liberal Party.

For the inter-war years there are two main debates. One seeks to explain why the Labour Party was able to maintain its position as the second party in the British parliamentary system, despite the problems which it faced in organising the local constituency parties. Christopher Howard has argued that the Labour Party's prospects and hopes in the 1920s were as 'Expectations born to death', and that the Labour Party would have been less successful had its political opponents realized how weak its party organization was.[3] On the other hand, recent writings have suggested that the Labour Party was developing quickly, that its organizational activities abounded, and that given the over-whelming support which it received from the working class the strength or weakness of its organization was, in any case, something of an irrelevance. The other debate concerns Ramsay MacDonald's 'betrayal' of the second Labour government in 1931. It seeks to explain why MacDonald, Labour's aberrant leader and possibly the most reviled political figure in twentieth-century British politics, left the Labour Government in August 1931 to form a National Government. The animus which MacDonald's action created has divided historians between those who simply dismiss his actions as treachery and those who believe that he had just cause for the course of action he followed.

For the years between the early 1940s and 1951, there have been two controversies surrounding both the achievements and the image of Labour. The Attlee administrations have figured prominently as historians have tried to measure both Labour's contributions to the development of the welfare state and the divisive nature of the development and control of the health service. Was Labour simply implementing the policies outlined in the Beveridge Report, offering souped up Liberalism, or was it making a genuine attempt to offer socialism and citizenship to all? In addition, the reasons for the Labour Cabinet's division over the National Health Service between 1949 and 1951 have been hotly debated between those historians who see the attempt to impose health charges as evidence of the lack of socialist commitment by the Labour Government, and others who see the issue as a relatively minor one which in no way undermines the socialist achievements of the Attlee years.[4]

All these debates have been subject to numerous interpretations, though four distinct approaches, or 'schools of thought', are evident. Historians of the Liberal Party, such as Roy Douglas, Trevor Wilson and P.F. Clarke, have questioned the assumption that the Liberal Party was losing out to Labour before the First World War and, though they express a considerable range of ideas, conclude that there was nothing inevitable about the 'forward march of Labour' or, indeed, the decline of Liberalism.[5] The revival of Liberal and Alliance fortunes in the 1980s has strengthened this school of thought in its conviction that it was the War which led to the self-induced division of the Liberal Party and that even this had not proved terminal. Labour's growth was thus seen to be accidental and not necessarily permanent.

A group of 'Labour' historians, which includes Ross McKibbin and James Cronin, tends to see Labour's growth as being potentially inexorable.[6] This is, in part, a revival of the ideas put forward by G.D.H. Cole and the Webbs and maintains that the extension of the franchise to all the working class, plus the emergence of class voting, led to Labour's inter-war growth. By the 1920s, Labour was the party of the working class. In essence, it is argued that Labour developed in the first half of the twentieth century because of class politics.

Marxist historians provide a third framework for the study of Labour history. Although there are immense variations between different shades of Marxist opinion, the one dominant theme which emerges is that the Labour Party has constantly failed to offer socialism to the British electorate. There is often a touching faith that if it had done so then its political success would have been assured, though this view is often tempered by the further assumption that there is nothing to be gained from working through the parliamentary system. This strand of thought is also evident in Ralph Miliband's book *Parliamentary Socialism*, which has highlighted Labour's withdrawal from socialism since 1918, and even in the writings of David

Howell, whose reference to 'Ramsay MacKinnock' captures the essential pessimism of some writers towards ever reaching socialism with a British Labour leadership which is prone to compromise.

Marxist historians have, of course, disagreed about the precise course of British Labour history in general and the role of the Labour Party in particular. Although the 'peculiarities of the English' debate of the mid-1960s was wider than simply a discussion about the Labour Party it had repercussions for attitudes towards it. In the debate Perry Anderson and Tom Nairn rejected E.P. Thompson's romantic and heroic vision of the working class shaping its own history. In its place, they argued that working-class history was determined by the ruling class.[7] Since then the work of Gramsci has been widely used to suggest that the working class are manipulated by the ruling class. But Gramsci held out hope for socialism for he distinguished between the state and civil society – which was the accumulation of voluntary activities and associations, trade unions, churches, community, political parties and trade unions. In societies such as Britain, where civil society was highly developed, he argued that the advance of socialism consisted of the transformation of the civil society as the basis for the transformation of the state. The implication is clear; the Labour movement could only work within the framework laid down by the ruling class but could achieve socialism, if it wished, through a moral and intellectual crusade in civil society. Indeed, it has been argued that the creation of the welfare state in post-war Britain might be viewed as evidence of the success of building a consensus between a diverse set of social forces in order to transform the state.[8]

A fourth set of opinions, offering an empirical approach, is influenced by the work of R.F. Price who believes that there is nothing inevitable about the course of Labour history.[9] He maintains that, whether in industrial relations or politics, the Labour process in society has worked through a constant series of accommodations and negotiations, conditioned by the social and economic environment, which as circumstances change may set off a further series of compromises. For Price, then, it is a normal situation for Labour's forward march to be halted and reversed: there is nothing certain about its growth if the conditions change. Equally, there is nothing unusual about the secret MacDonald–Gladstone pact, the Lib–Lab pact, of 1903.

In sum, then, four approaches have dominated the historiography of the Labour Party. To 'Liberal' historians and to some empiricists there is nothing inevitable about the rise of the Labour Party. The First World War, and any variety of factors, could encourage or delay its growth. To Marxist historians, the Labour Party is not likely to achieve socialism, though it might occasionally form a government. Only the McKibbin and Cronin approach exhibits the almost Whiggish belief in the inevitable progress of the Labour Party.

Yet, whatever the interpretations of historians, it is clear that the Labour Party experienced major, though by no means uninterrupted, political growth in the early twentieth century. This appears to have been the product of two major factors. The first is that, despite the influence of socialist groups, the early years of British Labour politics were dominated by Liberal Radicalism. The early Labour leaders – Keir Hardie, Philip Snowden and Ramsay MacDonald – were raised in the political atmosphere of Liberal Radicalism which committed them to the belief in the inexorable path of progress and made them fervent advocates of Gladstonian economic orthodoxy, with its emphasis upon free trade and balanced budgets. It is wise to remember that the Labour Party did not adopt a socialist clause until the 1918 Constitution was introduced and that even then Liberal Radicalism prevailed within the Labour leadership and dominated the policies of the first two Labour governments in 1924 and 1929–1931. It was not until the departure of Philip Snowden and Ramsay MacDonald in 1931 that Liberal Radicalism fully gave way to other forces.

Secondly, and even more important, trade unionism became the increasingly vital factor in the success of the Labour Party. The whole purpose of forming the Labour Representation Committee in 1900 was to win trade-union support for the Liberal Party. By 1909, when the Miners' Federation of Great Britain affiliated to the Labour Party, this task had been largely accomplished. The trade unions provided the finance and membership for the Labour Party and dominated it with their huge affiliated membership. The 1918 Constitution further strengthened the trade-union hold on the party and this was extended through the inter-war years and after. There were obviously advantages for the Labour Party in this relationship as trade unionism acted as Labour's *modus vivendi* for obtaining working-class support. Indeed, the inter-war years saw class politics at its height, largely as a result of this relationship. But there were problems. Local constituency parties began to react against the domination of the trade unions. There was also much frustration at the relatively right-wing policies which trade unions exhibited. But most of all, despite their general support for MacDonald and the Labour leadership, trade unions posed a threat to the vision of a Labour Party commanding the support of all the classes – a vision which MacDonald and Snowden strongly supported. This conflict between the Labour leadership and Labour's trade unionists, partly explains why the Labour leadership was hesitant in speaking out in favour of the General Strike in 1926. Above all, it provides at least the context of the crisis of 1931 which saw the departure of Mac-Donald and Snowden, Labour's class of 1906, from the second Labour Government.

Given that the Labour Party has only really developed in the twentieth century, it is hardly surprising that it is only in the last fifty or so years that historians have begun to write its history and interpret its development. Indeed, it was not until George Dangerfield wrote his book *The Strange Death of Liberal England* in the mid 1930s that anything approaching an interpretation of the emergence of the Labour Party was offered. There were other, more specific, books which outlined the history of the Party, such as L. MacNeill Weir's *The Tragedy of Ramsay MacDonald* (1938), but they often had a specific purpose in mind. In the case of Weir's book that purpose was to villify MacDonald for implementing his 'long-thought-out-plan' to ditch the Labour Government in 1931.[10] It was almost obligatory that books of this era should be general and national in approach, concerning themselves with 'high politics' rather than low, rank and file politics. In Weir's case, his main evidence was rumour and innuendo, supported by the deliciously iconoclastic Low cartoons. In Dangerfield's case, the book is mainly a literary confection of assertions gathered around the view that the Liberal Party was incapable of dealing with the challenge of Labour.

It was another twenty years before Henry Pelling produced his seminal work *The Origins of the Labour Party* (1954). The significance of this work is that it moved the study of Labour history from the national to the local scene for, in commenting upon the early actions of the Independent Labour Party it was clear that the focus of attention had to move from London to the provinces.[11] This point was further emphasised by E.P. Thompson in his seminal article 'Homage to Tom Maguire', which offered an explanation of the growth of the ILP and early socialist groups based upon a study of the textile district of the West Riding of Yorkshire.[12]

In the last thirty years there has been much more detailed local research than ever before, including P.F. Clarke's *Lancashire and the New Liberalism*, and K. Laybourn and J. Reynolds's books on *Liberalism and the Rise of Labour, 1890–1918* (1984) and *Labour Heartland* (1987), both of which deal with the Labour movement in the textile district of West Yorkshire. There have been numerous articles dealing with the local ILP and Labour Party activities and the whole emphasis of Labour's history has been taken further from institutionalised to rank and file Labour history by the History Workshop movement which began to produce its journal, *History Workshop*, in 1976. Nevertheless, there are still only a handful of detailed studies of constituency Labour parties, such as David Clark's *Colne Valley: Radicalism to Socialism* (1981), and there is still a large void in our understanding of both regional and local Labour history, especially for the years since 1918.

Yet the change in emphasis and direction reflect the increasing availability, and widening range, of sources for the study of Labour history. In the last fifteen years or so new material, including constituency party records, government records, diaries, papers and letter collections have been added to the increasing availability of the records of the national Labour Party. In addition, more Labour Party papers and journals have found their way into local libraries in original and microfilm form.

The most obvious source of Labour records is the Labour Party itself, which has an archives department at its headquarters at Walworth Road, London, which contains an extensive collection of pamphlets, minutes and correspondence. Many of the most important of these have been reproduced, in microfiche and microfilm form, by Harvester Microform of Brighton, Sussex. Most notably, they have produced microfilm copies of the Labour Representation Committee correspondence 1900–1907, and microfiche copies of the minutes of the National Executive Committee of the Labour Party.

Unfortunately, the records of local Labour parties are far less rewarding, though they have become more available over the last decade. In theory every branch, every ward branch, and every town and constituency party ought to have minutes and other records. In reality, many of these have been lost through destruction or through secretaries not returning their records to the party. Only in a few cases have the records been deposited in local library archive collections. The ravages of time and individuals can be seen clearly in the case of the Leeds Labour Party. Although the surviving records of the Party were retrieved and placed in the local archive collection, only the records of the City Labour Party and one constituency party are extant; Leeds had one City Party, six constituency parties, 28 ward parties and numerous other local party branches after 1918. In other cases, such as in Huddersfield and Colne Valley, the records are fuller, though even in these cases only about half the relevant material survives.

In recent years both Harvester Microform of Brighton, and E.P. Microform of Wakefield, have recorded both local ILP and Labour Party records on microfilm, though the latter's Labour Party series, edited by Dr David Clark MP, has probably ceased to produce owing to the lack of suitable surviving records. Notwithstanding these difficulties, and in an attempt to preserve and locate what is left, Stephen Bird, the Labour Party's archivist, organised a recovery and retrieval system for Labour Party records in May 1988.

The deficiency in the Labour Party's local records is partly offset by the proliferation of local party papers which added to the publicity and propaganda work conducted by the *Daily Herald*, the Labour Party's national paper after the First World War. Most areas had a Labour paper of sorts and the heartlands of Labour power often had several. The West Yorkshire area was fortunate in this respect. At the end of the First World War it had three established provincial Labour papers. There was the *Bradford Pioneer*, the *Leeds Weekly Citizen* and the Huddersfield *Worker*. The *Worker* expired in 1920 but the *Huddersfield Citizen* replaced it in 1926 and survived up to the 1960s. In addition, there was the *Yorkshire Factory Times*, established in 1889, which acted as the weekly paper of the Yorkshire textile workers until it ceased publication in April 1926.

Like all Labour Party records, the Labour newspapers were a conscious and partial source – if anything even more emphatically committed to propaganda since these were often the only source of information for the vast majority of people who voted Labour.

This was blatently evident when the *Bradford Pioneer* advised its readers:

> Don't destroy this paper. Lend it. Become a Pioneer Pusher. Persuade your friends and workmates to order it. If YOU can sell a few in your workshop let us know and we will send them along. New readers means the extension of Labour's influence in world politics. 'Nuff said'. Get busy.[13]

Our knowledge and understanding of the Labour Party has also been greatly extended in recent years by the increased access to public and government records. For Labour historians there have been two major developments. First, the passage of time and the changing rules about the release of government records now mean that the Cabinet Conclusions and the Cabinet Papers of the MacDonald governments of 1924 and 1929–1931 and the Attlee governments of 1945 to 1951 can now be consulted in the Public Record Office. Although some items have been withdrawn as too politically sensitive, and will not be available until the twenty-first century, it is clear that this rich vein of evidence gives a clearer idea of the actions of the Labour Party in office.

The second development has been the tendency of politicians to deposit their private collections of letters, diaries and other material with libraries. The private collections of most of Labour's prominent politicians have been so deposited. The vast MacDonald collection, in the possession of David Marquand for about ten years, was deposited in the PRO in 1977. It contains the immensely valuable MacDonald diaries of 1910–1937, upon which this document collection draws. The Attlee papers are to be found in both Oxford and Cambridge university libraries and colleges. The Dalton papers, now edited and published in two splendid collections by Ben Pimlott, are in the British Library of Political Science, London School of Economics. The Glasier papers have been deposited in Liverpool University Library.

The difficulty with the records of all these politicians is that whilst they offer an insider's view they are conscious accounts of the thinking and attitude of the particular person. There is always the element of the self-fulfilling prophecy about them. Yet this is as nothing compared to the recent trend of politicians to publish their diaries and autobiographies.

The diaries and accounts of participating politicians are one of the most useful, yet one of the most partial, of sources. In recent years there have been many instances of the instant, 'sneer and tell all', type of diary. The Crossman diaries, the Castle diaries, and many others, have provided a good indication of what has happened behind the scenes in Labour politics.[14] But readers must be sceptical of the big self-serving element of these accounts.

Political diarists are always participants, or close observers, of what they describe. The very nature of their contribution is that of having a very personal interest in the events they cover and of protecting their own reputations. The later publication of diaries often allows the authors the benefit of hindsight, which might allow them to hide both accuracy and truth.

The relative decline of the Labour Party since 1951 and its dramatic collapse in the 1980s have been the cause of much revived interest in its early history – partly in the hope that such investigation might provide clues as to the possible reasons for its decline and suggestions for its future revival. In the late 1970s Professor Eric Hobsbawm posed the question – has the forward march of Labour been halted? In an attempt to answer this both Richard Price and James Cronin, in books already referred to, have offered their assistance, and Kenneth Morgan and Henry Pelling have revived optimism by their stirring accounts of the success of the Attlee years. Even Tony Benn has enthused about the success of the administrations and called for a return to the values, principles and commitments of 1945. Stirring stuff as it is, nostalgia does not resolve the current problems of the Party – though it has served to stimulate the production of various interpretations of the history of the Labour Party during recent years, many of them unashamedly partisan in approach.

This penchant for the re-examination of Labour Party history has been greatly facilitated by the availability of new sources. The documents in this Reader indicate how the available primary sources now offer more varied viewpoints and explanations of events than was once the case. Their range suggests how Labour history has, in recent years, moved from the institutional type of history, which located itself in the national movement and the chief events which shaped the contours of its history, to the more rank and file approach. Most certainly the increasing availability of new and more varied sources has enlivened and enriched the various debates which have dominated the history of the Labour Party – and it is debate which is the very substance of history.

NOTES

1. M. Foot, 'Ramsay MacDonald', review article of D. Marquand, *Ramsay MacDonald*, in *Bulletin of the Society for the Study of Labour History*, 35 (1977), p. 70.
2. G. Dangerfield, *The Strange Death of Liberal England* (London, MacGibbon & Kee, 1966 edition), p. 22 and chapter two.
3. C. Howard, 'Expectation born to death: local Labour Party expansion in the 1920s', in *Working Class in Modern British History: Essays in Honour of Henry Pelling* (Cambridge University Press, 1983), edited by Jay Winter.
4. H. Pelling, *The Labour Governments 1945–1951* (London, Macmillan, 1984); K.O. Morgan, *Labour in Power 1945–1951* (Oxford, Clarendon Press, 1984).
5. P.F. Clarke, *Lancashire and the New Liberalism* (Cambridge, Cambridge University Press, 1971); T. Wilson, *The Downfall of the Liberal Party 1914–1935* (London, Collins, 1966); K.D. Brown, *The English Labour Movement* (London, Gill and Macmillan, 1982); K. Burgess, *The Challenge of Labour* (London, Croom Helm, 1980); R. Douglas, 'Labour in Decline 1910–1914', in K.D. Brown, ed., *Essays in Anti-Labour History* (London, Macmillan, 1974); M. Bentley, *The Climax of Liberal Politics: British Liberalism in Theory and Practice 1868–1918* (London, Edward Arnold, 1987).
6. J.E. Cronin, *Labour and Society in Britain 1918–1979* (London, Batsford Academic and Educational, 1984); R. McKibbin, *The Evolution of the Labour Party 1910–1924* (Oxford, Oxford University Press, 1974).
7. P. Anderson, 'Origins of the Present Crisis', *New Left Review*, 23 (1964); T. Nairn, 'The English Working Class', *New Left Review*, 24 (1964).
8. *Marxism Today*, April 1987, Gramsci Supplement.
9. R. Price, *Labour in British Society* (London, Croom Helm, 1986).
10. L. MacNeill Weir, *The Tragedy of Ramsay MacDonald* (London, Secker and Warburg, 1938), p. 383.
11. H. Pelling, *The Origins of the Labour Party* (London, Macmillan, 1954).
12. E.P. Thompson, 'Homage to Tom Maguire', in A. Briggs and J. Saville, eds., *Essays in Labour History* (London, Macmillan, 1960).
13. *Bradford Pioneer*, 7 March 1919.
14. B. Castle, *The Castle Diaries 1974–76* (London, Weidenfeld and Nicolson, 1980); R.H.S. Crossman, *The Backbench Diaries of Richard Crossman*,

ed., J. Morgan (London, Book Club Association, 1981); H. Gaitskell, *The Diary of Hugh Gaitskell*, ed., P.M. Williams (London, Jonathan Cape, 1983); H. Dalton, *The Political Diary of Hugh Dalton, 1918–1940 and 1945–1960*, ed., B. Pimlott (London, Jonathan Cape, 1987); H. Dalton, *The Second World War Diary of Hugh Dalton 1940–45*, ed., B. Pimlott (London, Jonathan Cape, 1986).

SOCIALISM AND TRADE UNIONISM 1881–1900

It was not until the 1880s, in the wake of local and parliamentary legislation which widened the franchise and removed many of the restrictions on candidates, that a politically independent Labour movement was able to emerge. In some cases, such as in Lancashire and London, the spark came from socialist groups, such as the Social Democratic Federation (1, 2, 3), a quasi-Marxist organisation. In Scotland it was the work and example of James Keir Hardie (10) which gave inspiration to the movement. In other areas, most prominently the West Riding of Yorkshire, stimulus came from the impassioned appeal of William Morris (3), the Socialist League and from a broad group of frustrated Liberal Radicals and trade unionists (9, 12, 15, 25) who came to believe that the Liberal and Conservative parties were not the political vehicles for achieving working-class aspirations.

In Bradford, the birthplace of the national Independent Labour Party in January 1893 (13, 14), a major dispute at Manningham Mills (9, 11) led to the formation of a Labour Union (later ILP) in 1891. This collectivist organisation captured the support of the Trades Council in 1892 and sponsored the unsuccessful parliamentary campaigns of Ben Tillett and Keir Hardie in the 1890s – eventually returning Fred Jowett for Bradford West at the general election of 1906.

In Halifax, the financial support of John Lister, a Fabian and owner of the Shibden Hall estates, and the considerable support of the Trades Council, led to the formation of the Halifax Labour Union in

1892 (12). Yet even though Halifax was one of the most important centres of independent Labour activity in the 1890s it was riven by deep divisions between its leading activists which led to some decline in its political achievements in the mid 1890s (25, 26, 27, 28). This conflict revealed that many local ILP branches considered themselves to be independent of the national organisation and were thus prepared to tell Keir Hardie to keep out of their affairs.

Despite the growing political support for the early Labour movement, there were political setbacks. The Halifax situation was simply a larger version of the type of conflict which occurred in many other areas. But there were also other factors which helped to explain the ILP's decline in the mid and late 1890s. The most important was the fact that all 28 ILP candidates in the 1895 General Election were defeated, an event which has been described as 'the most expensive funeral since that of Napoleon'. In the wake of that defeat, ILP membership began to evaporate and local political successes became fewer. During the next few years the movement was sustained largely by the development of a small hard core of support which hovered around the cultural activities of the movement. ILP clubs promoted social gatherings, book clubs, outings and cricket competitions. The Clarion movement encouraged the formation of vocal and glee unions, scouts, cyclist clubs and fellowship meetings. Labour churches and Socialist sunday schools, with their meetings and their message of fellowship, also aspired to 'make socialists'.

William Morris was the great initiator of this aspect of the work of the movement, although he eschewed the parliamentary activities of many socialist organisations (4, 5). In the early 1890s, however, it was John Trevor, an ex-Unitarian minister, who pressed forward Morris's ideas. With Robert Blatchford and Edwin Halford, Trevor founded the Labour Church movement, which offered lectures and 'services' for those who were interested in socialism. But the movement was short-lived, never being able to develop the theology which Trevor sought, and declined in the late 1890s as its leaders, particularly Trevor who had severe financial problems, failed to offer the clear lead which was necessary (6, 17, 18). Nevertheless, the Labour Church movement did help to sustain socialism through the difficult years of the 1890s (19). In some respects, it was replaced by the Socialist Sunday school movement which, between the late 1890s and the First

World War, offered fellowship and brotherhood to several thousand families through adult and children's classes on moral guidance, reading and Esperanto, the new language of international communication being developed in the late nineteenth century. The purpose of the Socialist Sunday schools was to make socialists, to win children to socialism, and to teach the moral values of goodness and brotherhood. Of the Socialist Precepts which the movement held the most important was the fourth which commanded children to 'Honour the good, be courteous to all, bow down to none' (20). It was a message which grew and was sustained until the First World War, when patriotic sentiment and conflict undermined and devastated all progressive thought which based itself upon peace, international brotherhood and fellowship.

These cultural developments kept the heart of the movement beating and the writings of Philip Snowden (21, 22, 23) are a reminder of the great emphasis which was placed upon the duty of the individual within socialism. Nevertheless, by the early twentieth century this cultural side of the movement was less relevant as trade unionists flooded into the new Labour Representation Committee, which drew the Independent Labour Party, the Fabians and the Social Democratic Federation into an alliance with the trade union movement, in February 1900. This proved to be a more durable alternative than the demands for unity between all socialists which emerged in the late 1890s and which would have excluded any alliance with a non-socialist trade union movement (29).

1) *Proposed Democratic Federation, 1881*
(Small SDF archive in British Library of Political Science, London School of Economics)
A few 'friends of Democracy' met at Westminster Palace Hotel with Joseph Cowan MP on 5 March 1881. They called a general meeting of London delegates on March 19 at which there were 150 people present. At this meeting they agreed that four main points would be put to a Conference of Delegates from all Societies in Great Britain to be held on 8 June 1881:

1st   Manhood suffrage for all Parliamentary and Municipal Elections
2nd   Triennial Parliaments

3rd Equal Electoral Districts
4th Payment of Members and all Election expenses out of the rates.

The following issues were also to be discussed:

1st Adult Suffrage
2nd Nationalisation of the Land
3rd Abolition of the House of Lords
4th Bribery at Elections to be made an act of Felony
5th Legislative Independence for Ireland.

DEMOCRATIC FEDERATION

At the last General Election held during a period of great public excitement, a vast number of members was returned to the House of Commons, who represent every interest in the country but that of the working class.

The result, so far, has been most unsatisfactory, and it has become necessary to frame a Social and Political Programme, which shall unite the great body of the people, quite irrespective of party in favour of those principles of justice, freedom, and steady progress, which are now too often set aside to suit the convenience of factions.

To secure at all times the fullest condition of the needs of the Working Class; to bring about economy in expenditure and simplicity in taxation; to urge on a complete re-organization of both Houses of Parliament, so that the business of the country may be efficiently done without infringing upon the independence of the legislature, are some of the broad objects of the proposed association.

In order to bring the genuine opinion of the country to bear upon Parliament, a thorough reform of the present Electoral System is demanded, so that the working classes may be enabled to send their own representatives to Parliament. By this means alone will the people themselves at last be able to direct all legislation towards the people as a whole. The miserable poverty, bad housing, neglected education (physical, moral and intellectual) of the general majority can never be appreciated or thoroughly reformed, save by those who have themselves suffered these evil effects. All taxation being raised from labour, the expenditure should be under the control of those who make the wealth of this, as of every country.

In purely political affairs, the Association would enter a protest against the injustice done to the loyal people of Ireland, by a most drastic Coercion Bill, which included retrospective clauses, obnoxious even to the least advanced of Continental Despotisms, as well as an Arms' Bill which practically suspends trial by jury for five years. These measures, carried in the interests of a handful of landlords, are directly opposed to the first principles of liberty. Justice to Ireland is a political necessity.

Throughout, the entire secrecy and indifference have been working harm to our fellow subjects whose interests are neglected in the strife of the parties. Full publicity and closer consideration are now essential.

In foreign affairs, owing to the mischievous old system of secret diplomacy, the people are left in ignorance of the policy which they may be called upon to back with their blood and their money.

At such a crisis at home and abroad, all classes of the people are invited with confidence to join in a vigorous organisation, which shall represent the opinion of many, and not surrender to the dictation of the few; which shall strive by existing local association, in every borough and every country, to obtain for all political representation and political power, and shall endeavour to base the management of the affairs of this great commonwealth on those principles of justice and freedom which have ever been dealt to the people of these islands.

By union alone can Englishmen, Irishmen, Scotsmen and Welsh-men ensure that their grievances will be redressed at home and no further wrong be done by their name abroad.

2) *J.L. Joynes to Fitzgerald of the SDF, about his campaigning for the SDF in Wales and Liverpool*
(Small SDF archive in the British Library of Political Science, London School of Economics)

> Dunies Decr
> Llandudno
> Aug 10 [1884]

To Fitzgerald,
I don't think you deserve an answer. What do you mean tantalising

me with no news? I opened it eagerly in the hope of gossip and scandal and squabbles, and find that I am to 'hear details when I get back'. I see from 'Justice' that liberties have been taken again with my name as usual. I gave Champion which he has apparently burked on the subject. I am about to change my name in consequence. This place is not one for propaganda. The scum of the rich Liverpool shopkeepers and their unspeakable wives and daughters disport themselves on the esplanade. The honest part of the population is at present employed in labouring for their various tastes in labouring for their various tastes in the way of dead animals and black-faced minstrelay. Besides nobody except these depraved scoundrels can speak English, and I cannot convert a Taffy without knowing Welsh. There is one blind man whom I have hopes of, as he sees more than most, but it is no use me giving him *Justice* unless you have it printed for the purpose in raised type that he can feel. I am sorry to be so discouraging, but it serves you right for sending me no news.

Yours very truly
J.L. Joynes

3) *William Morris campaigning in Bradford on behalf of the Democratic Federation, soon to become the Social Democratic Federation, in February 1884*
(*The Letters of William Morris to his family and friends*, ed. P. Henderson, letter dated 25 February 1884)

The Bradford lecture went off very well: a full house and all that: but they are mostly a sad set of Philistines there, and it will be long before we do anything with them: you see the workmen are pretty comfortable there because all the spinning and weaving is done by women and children; the latter go to the mill at 10 years old for 5 hours a day as half-timers: I don't think all my vigorous words (of a nature that you may imagine) shook the conviction of my entertainers that this was the way to make an Earthly Paradise.

4) *William Morris's letter to Burrows, December 1885, explaining his position and policy towards the SDF*
(SDF archive in the British Library of Political Science, London School of Economics)

19

Kelmscott House,
Upper Mill
Hammersmith
Dec 19 [1885]

Dear Comrade,

Thank you for your letter and the confidence you give me. As to the late discreditable occurrences & the consequent condition of the SDF there is at least one satisfactory circumstance in this, viz that such a large portion of the SDF feel them to be disgraceful & have the courage to declare their views in spite of any possible consequences. I and all those who left the Fed last year have always felt that the main part of the Fed was straightforward and sincere, though we may differ with them on some points.

As to my action in the present juncture, you must see that it is a matter of course that I can only act as a member of the Socialist League, the action that it determines upon I will support single-heartedly: but I may say, since I know it to be the general opinion, that we should make a great mistake if we attacked the Fed. On the other hand we should only be too glad to receive the adhesion of branches or individuals if they feel that they are doing no good in the SDF because it is being swayed in a direction contrary to their principles. Of course they could not join us unless they agreed with our openly expressed views and the tactics that necessarily came from this.

[Attacks *Justice*, the journal of the SDF] which clearly deserves to perish. [. . .]

William Morris

5) *William Morris expressing his opposition to parliamentary representation as a means of promoting socialism*
(Labour Party Archive, Walworth Road, London. Also in *Among Our Souvenirs*, Labour Party, London, 1975)

Kelmscott House,
Upper Mall,
Hammersmith.
Oct 14 1885

Dear Comrade

I send today Misery & the way out to begin with, and think it certainly would be the best way to copy it out; only it will gain you a pile of work. I need not say I trust you fully in the matter.

No, I wouldn't send men to Parliament, at any rate not at present: because now they would be helping it to prolong its existence and fulfil its formation of *class* government: but it may, and probably will happen that Parliament will get so disorganized that a strong body of Socialist thought break it up and get a vote appealing to a National Convention or some such thing. This certainly *might* give us the Command of the army, and would throw the burden of open violence on the reactionaries. However I am sure you will see that 'tis no use prophesying as to the details of the revolution. If we can only get a sufficient *opinion* behind us, it will dictate what action is to be taken. Two things I am sure of: if violence is inevitable it will be begun by the reactionaries; also they will not venture to try it on if we are strong & united. We have at present one thing to do to convince people that we are right, and that the change must come.

Yours Eternally
William Morris

6) *Thomas Cooper, ex-Chartist, writing to Mr. F. Pickles on the foolishness of pursuing his socialist activities and ideas.*
(Labour Party Archive, Walworth Road, London. Also in *Among Our Souvenirs*, Labour Party, London, 1975)

26, Ash Grove
Bradford,
Tuesday, 7 July, 1885.

My dear Sir

I do not know your age – but as the years I can expect to live are now few, I can only attend to my *one* work.

How many years you, my sanguine friend, expect to live, I cannot tell. But I must say to you, frankly & without hesitation, that if you could get a grant of life to the age of Methuselah, you would not see the programme of Socialism marked out in the pamphlet you have sent me, realised & established.

Such is my honest belief. It is for yourself to consider whether it will not be a waste of your existence to have anything to do with these Socialists. If you allow me to advise you, I would say, throw your energies into some plan, scheme, or project, for the benefit of mankind which is likely to be realised *while you live*.

Yours truly,

Thomas Cooper

Mr Pickles

7) *Tom Mann on Henry Mayers Hyndman of the Social Democratic Federation*
(T. Mann, *Memoirs*, pp.26–7)
In the early days of open-air propaganda – for he took his turn regularly at outdoor gatherings as well as indoor – his essentially bourgeois appearance attracted much attention. The tall hat, the frock coat, and the long beard often drew the curious-minded who would not have spent time listening to one in workmen's attire. Hyndman always gave the unadulterated Social Democratic doctrine, as propounded by the Social Democratic Federation. He never whittled down his revolutionary principles, or expressed them in sugar-coated phrases. He took the greatest delight in exposing the exploitation carried on by the capitalists, and especially by those who championed Liberal and Radical principles . . . He cleverly criticised the workmen listening to him for not being able to see through the machinations of those members of the master class, closely associated with the church or politics, or both. At almost every meeting he addressed, Hyndman would cynically thank the audience for so 'generously supporting my class'. Indeed, he brought in 'my class' to an objectionable degree. [. . .]

It was no small matter to know that in our advocacy of our principles we had learned to love, which on so many occasions brought forth stinging criticisms from the press, Hyndman's ability to state the case comprehensively, logically, and argumentatively was at our disposal always, and was of great value indeed. I am convinced, however, that Hyndman's mentality made it impossible for him to estimate the worth of industrial organisation correctly. For many years he attached no importance whatever to the trade union movement, and his influence told disastrously on others.

8) *The Fabian Programme, 1886*
(E.R. Pease, *The History of the Fabian Society*)
The Fabian Society consists of Socialists.

It therefore aims at the reorganisation of Society by the emancipation of Land and Industrial Capital from individual and class ownership, and the vesting of them in the community for the general benefit. In this way only can the natural and acquired advantages of the country be equitably shared by the whole people. The Society accordingly works for the extinction of private property in Land and of the consequent individual appropriation in the form of Rent, of the price paid for permission to use the earth, as well as for the advantages of superior soils and sites.

The Society, further, works for the transfer to the community of the administration of such industrial Capital as can conveniently be managed socially. For owing to the monopoly of the means of production in the past, industrial inventions and the transformation of surplus income into Capital have mainly enriched the proprietary class, the workers being now dependent on that class for leave to earn a living.

If these measures be carried out, without compensation (though not without such relief to expropriated individuals as may seem fit to the community), Rent and Interest will be added to the reward of labour, the idle class now living on the labour of others will necessarily disappear, and practical equality of opportunity will be maintained by the spontaneous action of economic forces with much less interference with personal liberty than the present system entails.

For the attainment of these ends the Fabian Society look to the spread of Socialist opinions, and the social and political changes consequent thereon. It seeks to achieve these ends by the general dissemination of knowledge as to the relation between the individual and Society in its economic, ethical, and political aspects.

9) *Extracts from the minute book of the Bradford Typographical Society, 1875–1893 dealing with the frustration of skilled trade unionists at the insensitivity of the Liberal Party on industrial relations and the Manningham Mills strike. There are also references to the demand for independent Labour representation*
(Minute Book of the Bradford Typographical Society, 1875–1893, deposited in the J.B. Priestley Library, University of Bradford by Mr. J. Reynolds)
Committee meeting held 23 October 1888.
It having been noticed from the imprints of the bills that many of the

Candidates at the Municipal Election were having their printing executed at unfair offices it was resolved:–

That a letter be sent (enclosing list of fair offices) to Candidates at the Municipal Election, asking them to give their printing to offices names on the list.

Committee Meeting held 13 November 1888.

That this Branch condemns the Candidature of Mr. Martin Field as a member of the School Board, he being an unfair employer and urges the members to oppose him in every possible way.

That if Mr. Martin Field goes to the Poll, the Branch officials be empowered to draw up a statement, print it, and placard it on the walls of the town.

Committee Meeting 19 November 1888.

Resolved:–

That, seeing that a working man Candidate had been adopted by the Liberal party, this Committee considers that under these alternative circumstances it would not be advisable to publicly oppose the Candidature of Mr. Martin Field, as specified in the resolution passed at the last Committee Meeting.

That a letter be sent to each Father of the Chapel asking him to request the members of the Chapel to make every possible means against the Candidature of Mr. M. Field for the School Board Election, he being an unfair employer.

Committee Meeting held at Market Tavern 10 February 1891.

That this Committee send a strong recommendation to the E.C. in support of the Strike hands at Messrs Lister & Co. Limited.

Quarterly Meeting held 4 April 1891.

Resolved:–

That a further sum of £20 be granted to the Manningham Mills Strike hands.

That the Secretary write to the E.C. urging them to send a further and more substantial grant for the Manningham Mills strike hands. Notice of Motion – That the time has now arrived when the Bradford branch should go in for a reduction of hours and an advance of wages. – Mr. Thos. Holmes.

Quarterly Meeting held June 25th 1892.

That this meeting desires to place on record its entire concurrence and approval of the action of the Bradford Trades and Labour Council in giving their moral support in favour of the candidature for the Western Division Bradford of Alderman Ben Tillett, who it regards as a faithful and earnest advocate and exponent of sound trade union principles.

10) *Keir Hardie's Election Address, Mid-Lanark, 1888*
(Quoted in E.J. Hobsbawm, *Labour's Turning Point*, pp.118–19)
At present the Members of Parliament returned from Scotland represent the following interests:

Landlords	18
Lawyers	21
Merchants	8
Shipowners	6
Army	5
Manufacturers	3
Schoolmaster	1
Doctors	2
Newspaper proprietor	1
Brewer	1
Various Learned Professors	6
	72

You will thus see that the working men of Scotland have not a representative to urge their claims. It is in order to remedy its admitted grievance that I now claim your support. . .

You are now in the position of men called upon to decide your own fate. Your lot in life hitherto has been hard and bitter. The commerical classes are now feeling keenly the effects of the poverty which has been yours for so long. Why is it that in the richest nation in the world those who produce the wealth should alone be poor? What help can you expect from those who believe that they can only be kept rich in proportion as you are kept poor?

'Few save the poor feel for the poor, the rich know not how hard
It is to be of needful food and needful rest debarred.'

I ask you therefore to return to Parliament a man of yourselves who,
being poor, can feel for the poor, and whose whole interest lies in the
direction of securing for you a better and happier lot. You have the
power to return whom you will to Parliament. I only ask you to use that
power as a means of securing justice to yourselves, by which you will
do injustice to no man.

11) *The Manningham Mills Strike, December 1890 to April 1891: a variety
of comments and reflections*

(i)   (*Yorkshire Factory Times*, 12 September 1890)

[Industrial relations had been bad at S.C. Lister's Manningham
Mills for a number of years and] it is becoming apparent that
from the multiplicity of labour disputes the mammoth establishment at Manningham is taking the lead, and the past year has not
in the number of wages and labour disputes, known or unknown
to the public, become less productive than its predecessors.

(ii)   (*Bradford Observer*, 17 December 1890)

[The management of the mills announced wage reductions of up
to 25 per cent on the 1,100 workers in the velvet department on
9 December 1890, to be implemented on 24 December. Allan
Gee of the Weavers' Association helped to organize the velvet
workers, and other groups who were affected by the threatened
reductions and helped to write and circulate 25,000 copies of a
Manifesto.]

In the face of these low wages we are of opinion that we should
be doing not only an injustice to ourselves but to the whole of the
textile industry in the West Riding of Yorkshire by accepting the
proposed reductions. [. . .] Help us fight against this enormous
reduction. Our battle may be your battle in the immediate future.
We trust, therefore, that in our present state of need and
disorganisation you will liberally support us.

(iii)   (*Bradford Observer*, 10 February 1891)

[From the outset, the strike leaders had no illusions of middle-
class support. W.H. Drew declared that they knew] perfectly
well that to a great extent the sympathies of the wealthier
Bradford citizens were not with the workpeople in the struggle to

obtain what they believed to be their rights. There were of course a few exceptions, and to these people every honour was due.

(iv) (*Bradford Observer*, 15 April 1891)

[The intransigence of the management to any form of negotiated settlement soon became apparent and a letter, in the *Bradford Observer*, an advanced Liberal paper, reflected upon this point.]

I can confidently assert that if the dispute had occurred at any other firm in the district, it would have been settled months ago; but it appears that Lister's, having determined to keep them there though all the business of the firm, and the money of the shareholders, be scattered to the wind. My knowledge of Mr. Lister through a period of forty years has led me to the conclusion that so long as he is allowed to lead all is well, but when once anyone becomes antagonistic to his ideas they must submit, when they prove their position equally as strong as his at all points.

(v) (*Bradford Observer*, 17 April 1891)

[As the dispute gathered pace, and all 5,000 workers at Manningham were on strike or were locked out, the need to hold large public meetings became important. However, the Liberal dominated Watch Committee of the Town Council attempted to prevent the strikers meeting in licenced accommodation and public places. This led to disturbances in Bradford on the 12 and 13 April 1891. On the latter the troops were called in and the Riot Act was read. The Central Division of the Liberal Party in Bradford, no doubt pushed forward by W.P. Byles, the advanced Liberal editor and owner of the *Bradford Observer*, passed a resolution condemning the actions of the authorities.]

That this meeting of the Liberal Central Division protests against the unjust action of the Watch Committee in refusing to permit the holding of a meeting on Sunday last in Dockers' Square, and regrets that by their action the authorities have instituted an invidious distinction, numerous meetings having been held there without objection or interference.

(vi) (*Bradford Observer Budget*, April 1891)

[The strike collapsed towards the end of April 1891, but such had been its impact upon the trade union movement and the local community that the very failure of the dispute encouraged some leading activists in Bradford to consider the need to form a political party for the working class, separate and distinct from the two major political parties. Indeed, it was Charlie Glyde, speaking at a meeting of the strikers in April 1891, who stated that] We have had two parties in the past; the can'ts and the won'ts, and its time that we had a party that will.

(vii) (*The Labour Journal*, 7 October 1892)
[The Manningham Mills made a profound impact upon Bradford society and the whole of the Labour movement. Many trade unionists, such as Ben Tillett and Tom Mann had given their help. Fred Jowett, who became the Independent Labour Party/Labour Party's first MP for Bradford in 1906, frequently reflected that the Manningham Mills strike helped to break the deferential attitude of the working class in politics and foreshadowed the end of the traditional two party system. Shortly after the end of the dispute he wrote the following.]

You have run this machine too long, we see the prejudicial results of your management – starvation, misery, crime, and a state of general unwashedness, body and soul, and we mean to take the matter in hand and try to make a better thing of it ourselves . . .

12) *The emergence of the independent Labour movement in Halifax*
(J. Lister, 'The ILP in Halifax' unpublished mss of 89 hand-written pages deposited in the Calderdale Archives, West Yorkshire Archives Service)
But 1891 saw a new spirit generating itself. In that year, a branch of the Fabian Society was established at Halifax of which Mr. Worsnop was, I believe, the main promoter. [. . .] I was invited by Mr. Worsnop, of Halifax, to attend a meeting of the local Fabian Society, which was being called in order to arrange for a lecture by Mr. De Mattos, entitled 'What is Socialism' on Tuesday, the 29 May. That gentleman . . . came to Halifax, delivered his lecture & stopped the night at Shibden Hall.

As a result of this lecture a Branch of the Fabian Society was established in Halifax, of which the Rev. Bryan Dale, M.A., was elected President. A course of lectures was also arranged. On the 18th

June, my Diary informs me,... I signed 'The Bases' of the Fabian Society and so became a full-fledged member. [...]

'The Courier' in its issue of August 1st, under the headline of 'Labour Representation in Halifax' informed its readers that 'The Trades and Labour Council are very likely to run two candidates in the Labour interest at the next (Municipal) Election in November. We understand also that a few candidates will be run for the School Board Election. We expect & believe we shall see now, that the Fabians have joined with the Trades & Labour Council, that vacancies on Public Bodies will be filled up by Labour men – even to the extent of one of the sitting MPs being removed, & a working man put in his place.'

I find in looking over my Diary that I was engaged, prior to & at this time, in reading up books dealing with the Labour movement & Socialism such as Kempner's 'Common Sense Socialism', Roc's 'Contemporary Socialism', and that exhilarating work by Karl Marx, entitled 'Das Kapital'.

On the same date, 13 August, a meeting of the Fabians was held at which it was settled to hold not only a course of lectures but also open-air Saturday meetings. Mr. Beever, the President of the Halifax Trades & Labour Council was present at this meeting – a man destined to lead & greatly aid by his efforts the Great Labour movement towards Independent action.

On 25 October, we were honoured by a lecture, at a meeting of our Fabian Branch, by Bernard Shaw – that pillar of Fabian Socialism – 'The Guardian' described him as one of the kid-gloved revolutionaries who pays this town an occasional visit with the object of disturbing social order, & sowing seeds of strife in a peaceful and contented community. [...]

An important step was taken at a public meeting at the Central Hall, in the first week of August 1892, when it was resolved that a 'Labour Union' should be formed for the town. This resolution was proposed by J.H. Beever & seconded by myself & a Committee to draw up the Constitution was appointed ... This meeting had been preceded by one held 26 July by the General Election Committee of the Trades & Labour Council when it was resolved to form a 'Labour Union' on democratic lines to take the political part of the Trades & Labour Council work, so as to allow that Council to devote its time to trade matters. About this time, these 'Labour Unions' were springing up rapidly in the cities & towns in Scotland & England, & we, in Halifax, were among the first & foremost in forming one, tho' Bradford boasts, or boasted, that the first of them all originated there. The Bradford Union had its inception in 1901 [1891], but was not, at first, I believe, definitely Independent.

Our 'Halifax Union' made great rapid strides, & had for its meeting place a room in Culver St. off North Parade, Mr. Tattersall was its first President. [...]

A Labour Meeting was held towards the end of Septre, in Shibden Park, at which addresses were given by Keir Hardie, MP, Peter Curran, George Cowgill, of Bradford Trades & Labour Council, F. Roper, J.H. Beever & J. Lister.

Mr. Beever made a notable speech in moving a Resolution in favour of the establishment of an I.L.P. party throughout the whole country. A similar Resolution was moved at a meeting in Halifax on the 18th Sept. by Keir Hardie in these words:–

'That this meeting of the workers of Halifax & district is of opinion that the time has come when a National & Independent Labour Party must be formed & thereby pledges itself to support an Independent Labour policy.'

[...]

The year 1893 was to see an event even more memorable in Labour Annals, viz; – the foundation of the National Independent Labour Party.

On Jany 13th & 14th of that year it was formed at a Conference held at the Labour Institute, Peckover St., Bradford. The delegates consisted of 121, of whom 94 were from Independent Labour organizations, 5 S.D.F. members, 12 Fabians, 4 from the Cumberland Workmen's Unions & 11 from 9 other organizations. At this conference Hardie was in the Chair.

A National Administrative Council, familiarly known as the N.A.C. was appointed consisting of Katherine St. John Conway; Dr. Aveling, son-in-law of Karl Marx; Pete Curran; Jos. Burgess; Alf Settle; Willm Johnson; W.H. Drew; J.C. Kennedy; Geo. S. Carson; & R. Chisholm Robertson; Mr. Shaw Maxwell being appointed Secretary, & myself Treasurer, ...

13) *Programme of the National Congress of the ILP formulated at the National Congress of the ILP at Bradford, 13 & 14 January 1893*
(Independent Labour Party, *Independent Labour Party 1893–1943: Jubilee Souvenir*, p.31)

Name –   Independent Labour Party.
Object –   The object of the Independent Labour Party shall be to secure the collective ownership of all means of production, distribution and exchange.
Membership –   No person opposed to the principles of the Independent Labour Party shall be eligible for membership.

PROGRAMME

Social
1. Abolition of overtime, piecework, and child labour under the age of fourteen years.
2. The restriction by law of the working day to eight hours.
3. Provision for the sick, disabled, aged, widows, and orphans, the funds to be raised by tax upon unearned increment.
4. Collective ownership of the land, and all means of production, distribution and exchange.
5. Free unsectarian education from school to the university.
6. Properly remunerated work for the unemployed.

Political
The Independent Labour Party is in favour of every proposal for extending electoral right and democratising the system of Government.

Fiscal
1. Abolition of indirect taxation, and taxation to the extinction of unearned incomes.
2. A graduated income tax.

14) *The naming of the Independent Labour Party*, 1893
(Independent Labour Party, *Report* of the foundation Congress of the ILP, p.3)

Mr. George Carson, Glasgow, moved that the title of the party should be the Socialist Labour Party. In Scotland the Labour Party had come to the conclusion that it was best to call a spade a spade.

Mr. R. Smillie, Larkhall, seconded the motion.

Mr. H.A. Parker, London, moved as an amendment that the title of the party should be the Independent Labour Party of Great Britain and Ireland. He said that they had to appeal to the vast mass of workers outside, and not only to Socialism. It would be a pity if they narrowed their party in the slightest degree by making it appear that they admitted only *bona fide* Socialists.

Mr. Settle, Manchester, seconded the amendment.

Mr. Wolfe, Colne Valley, said that the Labour Parties in Germany, France, America and in every country where those parties had been most successful were called Social Democrats – everywhere except England.

Mr. J. Burgess, London, said whilst he sincerely hoped it would not be supposed that anybody in that Conference was anti-Socialistic, it was perfectly clear to him that to demand a declaration as a Socialist from all the members of the party would merely be to stop the development of the army of workers, upon whom they were relying and ought to rely.

15) *Why I Joined the ILP*
(*Why I Joined the Independent Labour Party: Some Plain Statements*, ed. J. Clayton)

A.R. Orage [of the National Union of Teachers and later editor of *The New Age*]. Well, you see, I joined first and found out why afterwards. Most people flatter themselves that they look before they leap; as a matter of fact, very few people indeed look until they have leapt;. . . Nature is too wise to make men too wise, and it is only in Life's unimportant details, such as choosing a cigar or electing an M.P., that she allows us a chance of bungling. Logic is her invention to delude us into thinking we think, and we show our just appreciation of its value by preferring Instinct to Reason and first impressions to anything else. [. . .] I joined the I.L.P. because I felt it the right thing for me to do: I continue in the I.L.P. because I know it is. The feeling, however, came first, and the reasons, in plenty, came afterwards.

Isabella Ford [the daughter of a Quaker businessman who helped to organize the Leeds tailoresses in the late 1880s and early 1890s and became a leading figure in the Leeds ILP]. I was thinking of leaving the Trade Union movement altogether for the antagonism between men and women was widening, and I could see no way of interesting women in the movement. [. . .] Gradually I became aware of a stirring and lifting of the gloom. A possibility, perhaps even a probability, seemed growing that women and men should stand together as equals, in the industrial world and even in the political world.

Trade unionists I found, were beginning to preach that women must join because they were human beings. Women, it was said, were men's friends and helpers in the industrial world.

I read a political manifesto in which adult suffrage was a foremost plank, – and in a municipal programme, it was declared that women ought to sit on Town Councils. [. . .] and so I joined the I.L.P.

My last doubts were removed after a visit to a Labour Club in the Colne Valley, when the men had been giving a tea party to the women and had poured out the tea, cut the bread and butter, and washed everything up, without any feminine help and without any accidents!

Arthur Shaw [President Leeds Trades Council, Hunslet Board of Guardians, and the Parliamentary Candidate South Leeds]. My reasons for joining the I.L.P. are the same that have induced thousands of Trades Unionists to cut themselves adrift from the orthodox Political Parties to work out their own social and industrial salvation. Previous to 1890 I had worked with ardour and perseverance for the success of the Liberal Party in Leeds, believing them to be the friends of the workers. We had just returned, for the South Ward of Leeds, a Liberal Councillor, a professed friend of Labour, when the gas-workers justly demanded an Eight Hours' Day. To this demand my friends the Liberals opposed a strenuous resistance, as a proof of their friendship, and imported into the town the scum of labour from all parts of England.

My particular friend of the South Ward entertained them at the Town Hall with 'Britons never shall be slaves'. Other Liberals provided them with beer and tobacco, while at the same time the Leeds gas-workers were provided with military help, as another mark of Liberal friendship. This decided me. I vowed I would never again assist either of the Political Parties, and every day I become more convinced that my course was right. [. . .] In future politics must deal with the industrial problems, municipally and nationally, with Labour and with the conditions of labour, above all with National Product and

Co-operation. Hitherto, manual workers have received little or no attention beyond repression, but with the growth of national ideas and the ballot-box they will be able to command the attention they deserve. [. . .]

In face of the fact that in the House of Commons such Bills as the Employers' Liability Bill, Eight Hours' Bill, Prohibition of Married Women's Labour, Half-Time Labour, and other measures of equal importance to the vast majority of our people, were, and are, treated with 'marked indifference', I am of opinion that our Trades Unions must abandon begging, ánd by a policy of independent action, demand and enforce the radical alteration of present labouring conditions.

It is because I believe that such legislation can, and must be carried out by the workers themselves that I have joined the I.L.P., and in the belief that this movement will gradually lead to collectivist action, and so abolish the anomaly of overwork and no work, to pave the way to Universal Brotherhood.

D.B. Foster [ILP political candidate for Holbeck Ward and later regarded as one of the great political figures in the Leeds ILP]. [. . .] A better system must be found, wherein all shall work for each and each for all: and then "we shall arrive". For love and care for all shall find expression in our laws, that he who toils may rest assured of life's bare needs, and some of joy besides.

Such inspirations come to thee for thy fulfilment . . . Then let thy dreams be deeds, and all thy life a never-ceasing effort, till Politics be purged, and wise and righteous laws be made the rule of earth wheron shall dwell true peace and universal brotherhood. And so my heart was moved to join a small struggling band whose sole supreme purpose is to give to all an equal chance to live and grow beyond what men have often been, mere slaves to grind, and grind, and grind, while others lived in ease and smiled upon them contempt. Therefore I joined.

16) *A letter from John Trevor to Edwin Halford, of Bradford, on the problems of setting up the Labour Church movement and Union* (Francis Johnson (ILP) Collection, 1893/49)

The Plantation,
Norwich
7.7.93

Dear Halford,

I send six more agenda papers. Am glad that you are going into the matter seriously.

The Constitution has been drafted in view of my inability to be President of the new Union. I cannot possibly go about the country. It is not merely a question of strength. It is a question of money. I am running into serious difficulties in the matter of livelihood, & how to get out of them I know not, unless getting out of the whole movement, at least as any practical & organising goes. I cannot say herewith what needs to be said on the point. I will make a full statement if my position and difficulties at the Conference.

To give me a footing in the Council, I propose to be its chairman. Even if for the sake of keeping in touch with the practical development of the movement, so as to be able to write for it & edit the 'Prophet', some such arrangement seems desireth. This will be for the Conference to decide. [. . .]

With regard to the Presidency, the best man I can think of is Kennedy of Carlisle. He is a fine all round man, & his position on the National Executive is a consideration. I have, however, said nothing about it. Can you suggest anyone better? [. . .]

I am proposing that the elected delegates to the Council should be called V. Presidents for the sake of public announcements of special services & meetings. At the same time, by annual retirement, they remain a democratic institution.

Brockelhurst objects to being appointed annually with other offices. Hence I have put all offices – President, V. Presidents, on the same footing. This will need consideration. I should have preferred all offices being appointed annually, but think it would be unwise to make a sole exception of the only one who is paid for his services. [. . .]

Let me know if you need more information. Suggestions will be welcome. I am not happy about things. [. . .] In many places the movement is languishing & drifting & I think, were I differently situated, I could bring them up to the front.

Sincerely
J. W. Trevor

17) *Letter from J. Trevor to J. Keir Hardie, 30 October 1893*
(Francis Johnson (ILP) Collection, 1893/118 (i))

LABOUR CHURCH UNION

John Trevor Chairman   Edwin Halford Bradford
Hugh H. Herford Treasurer   S.G. Hobson Cardiff
Miss R.M. Scott Pioneer Secretary   S. Hodgskinson Bolton
F. Brocklehurst BA General Secretary   J. Craig Kennedy Carlisle
                                         Rulow Macclesfield
                                         30.10.93

Dear Hardie,
[. . .] Centres like Bradford, where the local spirit is so noticeable, will give trouble. The very success of the movement will intensify it. True, gods will multiply and abound. Blunder after blunder will be perpetrated in the name of democracy. In the midst of which I trust to see you stand, assisted, but weakened. That you have a rough time ahead I do not doubt.

How, in the matter of publicity, can I help the movement? Will an open alliance with you do good or harm to the real life I want to help to develop within it? I wish to be able to speak on your behalf. [. . .]
                                J. W. Trevor

18) *Letter from Edwin Halford to James Keir Hardie, c. October 1893*
(Francis Johnson (ILP) Collection, 1893/187. The reference to Miss M.M. was one to Miss Margaret McMillan)

Labour Church, 27 Clough Street, Bradford
Memorandum

Dear Comrade,
I herewith enclose two letters from Trevor. [. . .]

You know the views I hold re Labour Church Movement, the absolute necessity of its active assistance, if the Labour movement is to become a success. The power that it contains for lifting the question from the low sordid level which it now occupies to a higher and nobler plane of thought, and generally importing that solidity, that sense of brotherhood of humanity as a whole without which the movement must at no very distant date collapse like a bubble pricked with a pin.

Give the constitution a little of your consideration, talk the matter over with Miss M.M. and she will perhaps forward any suggestions you may make to me ...

Remain yours faithfully,

Edwin

19) *The Labour Church in Halifax, 1897*
(*The Record*, July 1897)

On Sunday, May 30th, Tom Mann addressed a large crowd on Savile Park, some 5000 persons being present, the subject dealt with being the Trade Union Movement in France. He gave a graphic description of the various sections and societies, showing progress made during recent years. In the evening he addressed a crowded audience in the New Public Hall on 'Some agitators of the Old and New Testament.' On Sunday, June 6th, Philip Snowden of Keighley, was the speaker. His criticism of the orthodox parties and his appreciation of the genius of Socialism was well received by the audience. His address on the Sunday evening on 'Socialism and Christianity' was one of the most brilliant addresses on the ethical side of the question ever delivered in the New Public Hall. On Sunday, June 13th, Miss Jennie Elcum, of London was the speaker. This was her first visit to Halifax. A good evening, though the heat was very oppressive, a good audience assembled to hear her address on 'Socialism and Women'. On Sunday, June 20th, Gregory, of Manchester, filled the place of E.J. Hall, who is fulfilling 'Leonard Hall's' engagements owing to the indisposition of the latter. E.J. Sale, of Birmingham, occupied the platform on Sunday. His subject in the afternoon was 'The Problem of Poverty' and in the evening 'An hour with Shelley the Poet'.

20) *Socialist Sunday Schools: Aims, Objects and Organisation*
(National Council of British Socialist Sunday Schools, *Socialist Sunday Schools: Aims, Objects and Organisation*)

DECLARATION

We desire to be just and loving to all our fellow men and women, to work together as brothers and sisters, to be kind to every living creature and so to help to form a New Society with Justice as its foundation and Love its law.

SOCIALIST PRECEPTS

1. Love your schoolfellows who will be your fellow-workmen in life.
2. Love Learning, which is the food of the mind; be as grateful to your teacher as to your parents.
3. Make every day holy by good and useful deeds and kindly actions.
4. Honour the good, be courteous to all, bow down to none.
5. Do not hate or speak evil of anyone. Do not be revengeful but stand up for your rights and resist oppression.
6. Do not be cowardly. Be a friend to the weak and love justice.
7. Remember that all the good things of the earth are produced by labour. Whoever enjoys them without working for them is stealing the bread of the workers.
8. Observe and think in order to discover the truth. Do not believe what is contrary to reason, and never deceive yourself or others.
9. Do not think that those who love their own country must hate and despise other nations or wish for war, which is a remnant of barbarism.
10. Work for the day when all men and women will be free of citizens of one fatherland, and live together as brothers and sisters in peace and righteousness.

DECLARATION OF FIRST PRINCIPLES

Question (1)– What is our Object?
Answer – Our Object is to realise Socialism.
Question (2)– What is meant by Socialism?
Answer – Socialism means common Ownership and control of those things which we all need in order to live happily and well.
Question (3)– Why is Socialism necessary?
Answer – Socialism is necessary because the present system enables a few to enrich themselves out of the labour of the people.
Question (4)– How would Socialism benefit the people?
Answer – Socialism would benefit the people as wealth would then be produced for the use of all.

Question (5)– What is wealth and how is it produced?

Answer – Wealth is everything required to enable us to live and is produced by the work of hand and brain.

Question (6)– Will Socialism provide the opportunity of a healthy and happy life for all?

Answer – Yes. Under Socialism there will be neither idle rich nor unemployed poor, but all shall share in the work of the world and in the joy of life.

Question (7)– On what principle does Socialism rest?

Answer – Socialism rests on the great principles of Love, Justice and Truth.

Question (8)– How can we apply these principles?

Answer – Through cultivating the spirit of service to others and the practice of Mutual Aid, we can apply these great principles and so hasten the advent of Socialism.

AIMS, OBJECTS AND ORGANISATION

Socialism is a political and economic concept based upon the idea of service to and love of humanity. The more Love and Justice there is in one's outlook, the truer Socialist one will be.

The moral teaching of our schools is interwoven in economic history, our working and social existence, the suffering of our fellows and the desire to uplift life as we know it.

WE BELIEVE :

That morality is the fulfilment of one's duty to the community.

That civilisation cannot survive unless society is completely re-organised on a foundation of Love, Justice and Toleration.

That Socialism is something more than a political theory – it is a Way of Life, unhampered by dogma, either political or theological, and it is everyone's duty to use all available social forces and achieve this end.

That by teaching children to think for themselves and by giving them a conception of a new social and economic relationship, we prepare the way for the building of a Socialist Society.

The fact that in no schools at present outside our own body is the whole of our Socialist creed taught, created the necessity for our own Socialist Sunday School where the Socialist humanitarian outlook upon life may be presented. [. . .]

Our teachers are expected to bear in mind two principles:–
(a) That the prime object of our school is to make intelligent socialists.
(b) That the basis of Socialism comes from the understanding of the history of mankind.

We classify the children more or less on the basis of age. The method of dealing with very young children is to chat with them, show them picture books, sing with them and above all, try to see things from their point of view.

We begin with simple stories of kindliness, courage and self-sacrifice drawn from the literature of all peoples, following with stories which point to the essential facts underlying Society, namely, the production of food, clothing and shelter.

As the children grow older, we point out who owns the means of production: who produces the wealth: who owns the greater part of the wealth produced: and what the condition is of the workers as regards the necessities of life. We deal with the great social movements of the past by telling stories from history, especially of the common people. We show the children that benefits enjoyed to-day are the result of sacrifice and struggles by their forebears.

We then go on to consider whether the present system is one making for the good of all people, that is, whether it is fulfilling the true function of Society by securing for human beings the right to labour and to enjoy the fruits of their labour. [. . .]

SUGGESTED AGENDA

(a) Opening Greeting.
(b) Song.
(c) Roll Call (explanation of Builders' Roll).
(d) The Minutes of previous Sunday School are read and endorsed. The purpose is to train the observation and memory of the children for future usefulness.
(e) Song.
(f) Precepts and/or Declaration of First Principles, Texts, etc. These are a very important part of the school. They should not only be repeated by the children but their meaning explained and the children encouraged to discuss them.
(g) Items by children and/or 10 minute question and discussion.

(h) Song.

(i) Lesson (Lasting 20 minutes). (Children to be encouraged to ask questions).

(j) Intimations (including Birthday card greetings and good wishes to be sent to any scholar absent through illness).

(k) Closing song and Declaration.

21) *Philip Snowden expressing the view, held by many early socialists, that personal salvation through religion was not sufficient to save the world from social chaos. Those who found personal salvation had a duty to examine the social problems in order to lessen individual suffering and to realise the 'New Jerusalem' on earth*

(Philip Snowden, 'The Two Salvations', *Labour Prophet*, April 1898)

[. . .] But among those who are agreed that the object of salvation should be, not to save us from the consequences of sin, but from the committal of sin, there is a grave difference of opinion as to the means by which this agreed object is to be attained. We are all familiar with the man who tells us that he agrees with Socialism at every point but we are going the wrong way to secure it. We must begin with the individual; get the individual heart all right and then I suppose a perfect society will be spontaneously added unto it. It is a striking commentary on the limited capacity of average intelligence that such a charge as this can be urged against us, when all our missionary efforts are directed to the individual, are appeals to him to realise his individual power and his individual responsibility. We are entirely at one with those who see the necessity for individual regeneration, but we recognise that social evils are of such character as to be altogether beyond the power of even the regenerated individual to remove. The man who believes that personal salvation, improvement in personal character, is sufficient, stops short with the discovery of half the truth. The individual possesses the power, within certain limits, to mould his environment; the environment influences the character, though not wholly, yet to a very considerable extent. [. . .] It is the conditions under which the people are compelled by our industrial system to live which inevitably breed the class of people whose character we so much deplore. To change these conditions, which are preventing the individual regeneration of the masses, is the social salvation which it is necessary to preach and put into practice as the complement to the preaching of individual salvation. And by improving the condition under which the people live we make the work of individual regeneration easier and possible. [. . .]

That personal religion alone is not sufficient to regenerate the world our social chaos is a standing witness; and this failure applies not only to one only but to all the religions of the world. Such teaching has failed to recognise the necessity for a congenial soil and atmosphere in which the new-born aspirations of the individual must grow and flourish. The Christian Church of our country, especially since it became a victim to the Individualistic revival following the economic changes of three hundred years, has confined itself exclusively to the preaching of personal regeneration as the cure for all worldly ills, and it has therefore done nothing, unless by accident, for the social amelioration of the people. And it is not possible that it could be otherwise; for if we believe in Individualism, we believe that the individual is an all-powerful and independent being, and that he as within himself, or by individual help of God, the power to mould his own condition; and thinking this we must believe also that individual fault. [. . .] This alone is sufficient reason why personal salvation of churches can never regenerate the world. We want something more than sympathy or love. This the personal salvation will supply. We want the knowledge of how we can best help others. [. . .] It is the duty of all who claim to have found personal salvation to seek out the causes of these social evils and irregularities, and to try to obtain full salvation by making for themselves and for all humanity a material habitation where all that is best may have every encouragement to grow. [. . .] Personal Salvation and Social Salvation are like two palm trees which bear no fruit unless they grow side by side.

[. . .] I have found everywhere men upon whom the principles of Socialism have had a remarkable effect in the raising of their personal character. Socialism regenerated them in the truest sense. They have become better fathers, better husbands, better citizens . . . And this same spirit is everywhere at work thoughout the world. This is the Spirit of Truth come to lead us unto all Truth. Under the spell of its power the old men are dreaming dreams and the young men are seeing visions; under its influence all oppression and wrong must fall, for it will still go forward, conquering and to conquer, until it has brought down the New Jerusalem on the cities of the earth.

22) *Philip Snowden expressing his faith in the ethical and individual basis of socialism in his most famous lecture 'The Christ that is to be'*
(P. Snowden, *The Christ that is to be*)

[. . .] Salvation by the blood of Christ in the light of this knowledge means, not that that sacrifice is a substitute for sacrifice by others, but it is an example that only by such sacrifice can others be saved. And with this knowledge the individual consciousness is passing into the consciousness of the social life.

This law of sacrifice, this law of love, of association, of co-operation, is not only the foundation of Christian teaching, but it is the basis of all the great ethical religions of the world and of all schools of morality. Not by individual selfishness or national selfishness has the progress of the human race been advanced. Men who have sacrificed themselves for the sake of what they believed to be the truth, have been instruments by which succeeding generations have been raised to a higher morality and to a higher civilisation. [. . .] The religion of the future will recognise the unity of all men. It will have for its ideal the complete organic unity of the whole human race. And this religion will be a political religion. It will be a religion which will seek to realise its ideal in our industrial and social affairs by the application and use of political methods. If Christianity is to be of any use it must be applied to our everyday life, and the only way in which principles, either Christian or otherwise, can be applied to social and industrial conditions is through the agency of political means. [. . .] There can be no separation between politics and religion. Law makers and administrators are inspired by certain ideas, and if these ideas be not moral then the law and its administration will be immoral. We cannot have a healthy religious life side by side with a corrupt political system.

This ideal of religion as saving one's life in the common life; this new conception of politics as a means of realizing this religion; all this today may seem far away, but it is the only way in which individual and social salvation can be attained. And in spite of so much around us opposed to the coming of this kingdom of righteousness, there are signs on every hand of a great and righteous power at work in the world. [. . .] There are signs on every hand that this social spirit is being awakened. The individual is feeling the throbbing of a new social consciousness; the Sun of Righteousness is rising with healing in its wings. The Christ that is to be appears. And this spirit of Christ, of love, of sacrifice, is taking possession of men's minds, and under its inspiration, old forms, old institutions, old passions will disappear, and a new brighter social order will arise. It is the promised New Jerusalem. The horrible social conditions existing today – poverty on the one hand and riches on the other – arduous toil on the one hand, luxurious idleness on the other, these will give way before this divine impulse, and the poverty of the many and the luxury of the few will join hands in a union of contented happiness for all. The horrible social conditions of today cannot continue before the diffusion of this social spirit. [. . .] I see that old things have passed away, and all things have become new; I see this sordid struggle for material existence super-ceded by a social order in which men seek the gratification of their natural ambitions, not by the amount of tribute they levy on their fellows, but by the greatness of the service they can render to them;. . . I see an industrial order where every man for a fair day's work has a bountiful harvest, and abundant leisure when his necessary work is done:. . . But the only way to regain the earthly paradise is by the old, hard road to Calvary – through persecution, through poverty, through temptation, by the agony and bloody sweat, by the crown of thorns, by the agonising death. And then the resurrection to the New Humanity – purified by suffering triumphant through Sacrifice.

23) *Philip Snowden and the 'Individual under Socialism'*
(P. Snowden, *The Individual under Socialism*)
A common objection against Socialism is that a Socialist State would involve the sacrifice of individual liberty, and that there would be no opportunity for the satisfaction of individual ambition.

Socialism, it is urged by these opponents, considers only the satisfaction of mere physical needs. Socialism, they tell us, lacks the moral element, it ignores human nature, it is meat and drink and nothing more. Such an objection as this betrays an ignorance of Socialism and the Socialist movement which would be irritating if it were not amusing. 'Socialism merely meat and drink and material conditions and nothing more.' 'And were it so, surely is there not need enough today for a movement which seeks to provide these things for the millions who are lacking meat and clothing, and homes? With, according to the latest investigation made in an industrial English town, about 80 per cent of the working class living in houses which do not fulfil the bestest needs of health and decency; with 52 per cent of the working class families unable, by long hours of toil, to gain income sufficient to obtain enough food to satisfy the needs of the body. . .

But it is further urged that if such an organisation of industry could be established as would ensure work for all willing workers, and satisfy the physical requirements of all, that such an organisation would be obtained at the cost of all that makes life worth living. Remove the incentive of gain, and we are told the motive force of all progress would be destroyed. Socialism would reduce all to one dead level of mediocrity. The individual would lose his identity in a cast iron State. Men would be converted into mere machines, life would be intolerable servitude, the nation would be converted into one huge prison house. The great principle of Socialism, these objectors remind us, is Equality; and to ensure a condition of perfect equality would be the work and function of the State. Aye, the State – a monster more terrible in its strength and more tyrannical in its despotism than ever the genius of Frankenstein created. To ensure this condition of perfect equality, the State will allot to each individual his appointed task, and the whip of the State taskmaster will enforce its full discharge. Intellectual equality would be secured by depriving superior ability of all encouragement to excel, the mental condition of the lowest would be the standard to which all would be degraded to maintain a condition of perfect equality. The State would decide and direct the minutest details of each individual life. The work, the place of abode, the dress, the food, the home, the amusement, the recreation – all would be directed by the State, leaving the individual no freedom but to obey. [. . .]

What to-day under our much vaunted individual freedom, is the type of developed individual. If you would see the works of Competition, and the play of the Incentive of Gain, look around! You will find their monuments everywhere. Surely but it must be in grim irony we are told that Socialism will destroy individual liberty and close the avenues for intellectual development. Let those who fear that Socialism will destroy individual liberty and hinder her intellectual development go with their talk to the machine workers of our great northern towns, who are chained for eleven hours a day to a monotonous toil with the eye of the overseer and the fear of dismissal spurring them on to an exertion which leaves them at the end of their day's work physical wrecks, with no ambition but to restore their wasted energies at the nearest public houses. [. . .]

There can be no individual liberty where land, the absolute essential to a man's existence, is the property of a few, and is used by this few to dictate to the many the terms on which they shall be permitted to live. There can be no individual liberty so long as machinery which has been made by the associated labour of all workers become the property of a class, and is used by that class to keep themselves in idleness and to pay the workers wages by wealth taken from them. Under such a system, where the common needs of life are the object of a competitive struggle in which all goes to the victors, leaving nothing to the vanquished; in which sole object in life is to secure a monopoly of what all need so that by this monopoly one may get his fellows into his power to use them for his own selfish ends – under such a system there can be no individuality. [. . .]

Socialism means the elevation of the struggle for existence from the material to the intellectual plane. Competition for material things – which are limited in supply – must result in extremes of poverty and riches . . . But Socialism will raise the struggle for existence into a sphere where competition shall be emulation, where the treasures are boundless and eternal, and where the abundant wealth of one does not cause the poverty of another. [. . .] We have a command over natural forces capable of supplying every need without the necessity for arduous toil – a command which increases more rapidly than our capacity for its rational use. By the sensible organisation of industry all might be provided with the needs of a comfortable existence with the expenditure of a little time and labour. [. . .] Socialism will establish the moral conditions which are necessary for the development of true individuality, and the exercise of true liberty.

24) *Conflict within the Halifax ILP, 1894–1895*
[ILP branches were semi-autonomous bodies and often resented the intervention of national leaders in their affairs. This became apparent in the conflict within the Halifax ILP in 1894 and 1895. It was occasioned by the decision of John Lister, of Shibden Hall and Treasurer of the national ILP, not to contest his municipal seat again in November 1894. He objected to his ideas being cut and dried for him by the local branch. The affair was complicated by the actions of

another prominent Labour official, James Beever, who switched seats to Lister's old ward and was returned with Liberal support. In consequence, the Halifax ILP, dominated by Montague Blatchford, the brother of Robert, and Robert Morley, an engineer who became associated with Tom Mann's Worker's Union, attempted to remove Lister from the ILP. The situation was further complicated by the fact that Lister was friendly with Hardie who, along with the ILP, was deeply in debt to Lister. There was also some enmity between the Blatchford's and Hardie. In addition, Hardie's intervention on Lister's side provoked an avalanche of letters from Halifax activists, telling him to keep out of Halifax affairs. In the end, differences were resolved and Lister stood for the ILP at Halifax in the 1895 General Election. But in 1895 and 1896 Lister drifted away from the movement, Beever was expelled and James Tattersall, one of the critics of Lister and Beever, joined the Conservative party. The three leading figures of the early years of the Halifax ILP had left or been expelled by 1896 and the movement temporarily went into political decline.]

25) *Letter from John Lister to J. Keir Hardie, 22 December 1894*
(Francis Johnson (ILP) Collection, 1894/212)

Dear Hardie,
    Please don't bother your mind in the least about the money. I will keep the accounts separate. I am so sorry to hear that you are so out of pockets yourself re the Mid-Lanark contest.
    I hope the 'Leader' is beginning to pay its way.
    I am sure you will be sorry to hear of the further developments of Halifax. I can't understand it at all. I am sure I have never given any cause to the unkind things that are being said about me.
    I thought it wisest to take no active part in the 'Elections' (though I would have spoken at the Monday Meeting had not 'Nunquam' been Chairman) but I took no action at all against our candidates. But even to speak to Beever now is considered an unpardonable crime. I can not really be so one-sided as they want me to be. Please let me have your advice as to whether I ought to attend another meeting and undergo a second heckling or shall I send my resignation of membership . . . of course any advice you give will be considered confidential. [. . .]

Yours sincerely
John Lister

26) *Reply from Hardie to Lister, 25 December 1894, marked confidential* (Francis Johnson (ILP) Collection, 1894/212)

My dear Lister,

[. . .] I saw the *Halifax Courier* with respect of L.U. meeting and felt an amount of indignation therat never before experienced at anything connected with the movement & it was on this I meant writing you.

I have as little false dignity as any man & care not what abasement I suffer if the movement is helped thereby but I wd see Mont Blong, Dyche & Co in hell before I wd respond to their insulting request. I say this in the best interests of the I.L.P. Better far sink the whole business than have it live in this atmosphere of bigotry, suspicion, distrust and, I fear, malice.

Were I in your place I would write a brief note declining the invitation, & point out that they have already prejudged the case by deposing you from your position of candidate, and that unless the resolution were rescinded they were to consider your note as one of resignation of membership.

If this be done it will leave you free to join another branch, the London Central by preference, as it is made up of members from all parties of the country. It might be well to write to Tom Mann as Sec. protesting against the resolution already passed and appealing to the N.A.C. against being condemned. [. . .]

The upshot will probably be the severence of the H.L.U. from the ILP & for the present I see nothing better that could happen. If the spirit of the H.L.U. become general in the movement I for one wd clear out.

Remember – I reckon on for doing the big generous thing and retaining a membership somewhere. None of us can afford to allow our own feelings or desires to dictate our course of action. Never was the call of duty more urgent than now. If the I.L.P. movement fails God help England.

For the sake of God's poor we must save it.

[. . .] Remember the spite & spleen are only *local*. No man in the movement has, or deserves, a warmer corner in the hearts of the best men & women in it than yourself.

Yours fraternally,
Keir Hardie

27) *Letter from Robert Blatchford (Nunquam) to J. Keir Hardie, 26 December 1894, from 37, Savile Park, Halifax*
(Francis Johnson (ILP) Collection, 1894/214)

Dear Hardie,

[. . .] There is no danger of the party here going on the rocks. The Labour Union is one of the soundest and healthiest bodies of Socialists in England. It has come through an ordeal which is bound to be applied, sooner or later, to every branch of the I.L.P. It has resisted the insidious attacks of the Liberals and has cast out the weaklings and intriguers without injury to its stability. The *Labour Leader* and the N.A.C. have, by well meant but mistaken action, made the position of the union more difficult. But all will come right. To save any further blunders let me assure you first of three facts.

1. That before this trouble I had a very friendly personal feeling towards Lister and Beever.
2. That I have acted throughout purely for the good of the Great Cause, from no personal feeling, and wholly from the facts as supplied by the acts and words of Lister and Beever.
3. That I have never mixed with the men here, nor talked to them; nor written to them, nor pulled wires nor used influence. Neither have I listened to gossip or slander.

The action of the N.A.C. re Beever at Glasgow was grotesquely comic. I laughed when I heard of it. If you understood Beever as well as I do you would laugh yourself. As for Beever's triumph. He had been elected by Liberal votes – that is all. [. . .]

You think I am hard on Lister. I read Lister's own letter in which he said he could not submit his policy to the control of the Union, and I at once said that he was unfit to represent Democrats and ought to be expelled. That is all I have said against him so far. But his conduct since has obliged me to look upon him as what we call 'a wrong un'. I have a letter of his which is dishonest. I am bound to print it, and to answer it. John Lister is treasurer of the I.L.P. Well, he is going the right way to be cashed out of the Halifax Labour Union as a shuffler and a traitor. I am sorry, but there is only one way with such men. [. . .]

Robert Blatchford

28) *A letter from R. Morley, Halifax, to J. Keir Hardie, the editor of the Labour Leader, 1 January 1895*
(Francis Johnson (ILP) Collection, 1895/2)

Dear Hardie,

I am under a considerable amount of perplexity, to know why you should consider it your duty to enlarge the publicity of our Trouble in such a conspiciously unfair way; and to judge in so undemocratic a spirit. [. . .]

Let me now give you a short history of our trouble; for it has not come upon us in a night. Permit me to down here as a right an equal publicity for this statement as your own; for I contend that you have defrauded the Halifax Labour Union of the possibility of a fair & just judgement from your readers . . . [He then gives a detailed outline of the events which occurred in Halifax. The gist of his letter was that Lister had undertaken to accept the will of the majority when he agreed to stand as an ILP councillor, that there had been disagreements on the Town Council between the ILP representatives, and that it was out of these tensions that the situation which had led to Lister's unfortunate withdrawal from the municipal elections had occurred. It was Lister's decision, and his subsequent actions which had led to the resolution.] 'That John Lister would not again be our parliamentary candidate' . . . [. . .] 'A score of sound honest men, are better than 20,000 unreliables' so said Hardie in Halifax last June. We believe it still & are therefore safe. Hoping a sounder judgement may possess you, & a less prejudiced position may be assumed towards us.

Fraternally Yours
R. Morley

29) *The fight for Socialist Unity from the 1890s to the First World War*
[In the early 1890s William Morris, Robert Blatchford and several other leading Socialists attempted to encourage Socialist Unity, the union of the major Socialist societies which existed in Britain. Their efforts failed, for the Independent Labour Party was reluctant to submerge its differences with the Social Democratic Federation. There was also another, unsuccessful, attempt to unite ILPers, members of the Social Democratic Party (formerly Federation) and the Clarion movement between 1911 and 1914.]

(i) *Manifesto of the Joint Committee of Socialist Bodies issued by the Hammersmith Socialist Society, which included William Morris, the Social Democratic Federation and the Fabians.*

(G.H. Wood Collection, the Library, Huddersfield Polytechnic. Fuller details are to be found reproduced in E.P. Thompson, *William Morris, Romantic and Revolutionary*)

There is a growing feeling at the present time that, in view of the increasing number of Socialists in Great Britain, an effort should be made to show that, whatever differences may have arisen between them in the past, all who can fairly be called Socialists are agreed in their main principles of thought and action.

This is the more hopeful since, though much has been made of those differences by the opponents of Socialism, it is safe to say that they have been rather of less than more importance than similar disputes of the early days of great movements which have afterwards become solid and irresistible. [. . .]

The first step towards transformation and reorganisation must necessarily be in the direction of the limitation of class robbery, and the consequent raising of the standard of life for the individual. In this direction certain measures have been brought within the scope of practical politics; and we name them as having been urged and supported originally and chiefly by Socialists, and advocated by them still, not, as above said, as solutions of social wrong but as tending to lessen the evils of the existing *régime*; . . . The following are some of the measures spoken of above:–

An Eight Hours Law.

Prohibition of Child Labour for Wages.

Free Maintenance of all Women for Equal Work.

An Adequate Minimum Wage for all Adults Employed in the Government and Municipal Services, or any Monopolies, such as Railways, enjoying State Privileges.

(ii) *Robert Blatford and the 'One Socialist Party', 1894*

(*Clarion*, 22 December 1894)

The only hope of the emancipation of Labour lies in Democratic Socialism. A true Labour Party should therefore be a Socialist party. A true Socialist party should consist of Socialists, and of none others but Socialists. Now, the Independent Labour Party does not consist wholly of Socialists. It has now in its ranks very many men who are not Socialists. These men are a source of danger and weakness. I am perfectly convinced myself that the only cause worth fighting for is Socialism, that the only men likely to fight victoriously for Socialism are Socialists, and that the first and greatest work of all true Socialists to undertake is the formation of a united Socialist party. . . I desire to see one party, and I shall continue to advocate the formation of one party: but if it is formed it must be formed by the action of the members of the various existing bodies.

(iii) *The I.L.P. News summarizing the gist of Keir Hardie's opposition to the attempts to fuse the Independent Labour Party with the Social Democratic Federation, in 1896 and 1897*

(*I.L.P. News*, August 1897)

It may be that there is something in the methods of propaganda, if not in the principles, of the S.D.F. that not only renders it somewhat antipathetic to our members, but out of touch and harmony with the feelings and ideals of the mass of the people. If, too, it be the case that the S.D.F., even if not decaying, is not growing in membership, the indication would seem to be that it has not proceeded on the lines of British industrial evolution. It might be, therefore, that the introduction of its spirit and methods of attack would check rather than help forward our movement.

(iv) *Victor Grayson on the need to create a party of Socialist Unity, 1911*
(*Clarion*, 4 August 1911)

The psychological moment has at last arrived. . . The time for the formation of 'THE BRITISH SOCIALIST PARTY' has definitely come! If we miss the moment we have missed the opportunity of a century.

(v) *Victor Grayson campaigning for the British Socialist Party, 1911*
(*Clarion*, 11 August 1911)

On Saturday I addressed a magnificent meeting in Colne Valley, and at the close a resolution to the following effect was put to the meeting 'That in the opinion of this meeting immediate steps should be taken towards the formation of a united British Socialist Party.' The forest of hands that shot up in favour of the resolution was a beautiful sight to see, and there was not a single hand raised in opposition.

(vi) *Leonard Hall's attack upon Hyndman's advocacy of purely political tactics at the inaugural conference of the British Socialist Party, 1912, which helped destroy the unity of the organisation*

(*Clarion*, 3 May 1912)

The great defensive and destructive duties of Industrial Unionism must not be allowed to overshadow its essentially constructive function in the transition to Socialism. . . Under Socialism itself the co-ordinating centres would be Parliaments of Industry not Parliaments of Politicians. No free and self-respecting community would have any need or room for partisan 'Punch and Judy' politics.

THE LABOUR REPRESENTATION COMMITTEE AND THE LABOUR PARTY, 1900–1914

The Labour Representation Committee was formed in February 1900 in order to unite socialists and trade unionists in an attempt to form a viable independent political party for the working class. From the start, it deliberately pursued the policy of winning trade-union support – even to the extent of excluding any reference to socialism in its constitution (1, 4). Although its prospects looked bleak at first, it had been formed at a fortuitous moment in the development of trade unionism as a result of the Taff Vale case of 1900 and 1901, which eventually saw the House of Lords uphold an injunction from the Taff Vale Railway company permitting it to sue for damages from the Amalgamated Society of Railway Servants due to the strike action of some of its members. Following this, many trade unions recognised the need to protect their interests through the politics of the LRC. MacDonald's appeal for trade union support (2) was particularly apposite.

From the start, the LRC emphasised its independence from the other major political parties (5), though in reality J. Ramsay MacDonald, its leading figure, was always willing to make political compromises. His organisation had been formed out of an alliance between socialists and trade unionists. In 1903 he secured the secret Lib–Lab, Gladstone–MacDonald, pact which allowed LRC candidates a straight run against the Conservatives in up to 30 seats without Liberal opposition, or in conjunction with the Liberal candidate in two-member constituencies, in return for reciprocal arrangements for Liberal candidates (6).

The alliance with the trade unions and the Liberals paved the way for the LRC's parliamentary breakthrough in the December 1905 General Election, when it returned 29 MPs. Shortly afterwards the LRC changed its name to the Labour Party.

Yet not everyone was pleased and the euphoria of success was short-lived. The various compromises into which the LRC/Labour Party had entered created problems. There were local protests at the link with Liberalism (6 ii, 7). Victor Grayson stood in Colne Valley at a parliamentary by-election in 1907, although MacDonald opposed him due to the fact that Colne Valley was one of those seats which had been given to the Liberals in the 1903 Lib–Lab pact, and Ben Tillett was most critical of the ineffectiveness of the Labour Party in the House of Commons (9, 11) suggesting that 'the lion has no teeth or claws, and is losing his growl too'.

The problems of the Labour Party persisted, even though it had returned 40 and 42 MPs respectively, at the January 1910 and the December 1910 general elections; the increase had been due largely to the affiliation of the Miners' Federation of Great Britain to the Labour Party in 1909 which added mining MPs, who had previously been Liberals. The Osborne Judgement of 1909 (12) robbed the Labour Party of much needed finance by forcing trade union members to contract into the political levy arrangement rather than contract out, and the party organisation lacked clear unity and purpose (13).

Nevertheless, on the eve of the First World War, the Labour Party was still a powerful and expanding organisation, rapidly increasing its local and municipal representation. Its willingness to contest parliamentary by-elections (3) and to campaign on behalf of the unemployed (10) had established it firmly as the party of the working class and the major left-wing party in British politics. Its trade union membership had increased from 904,000 in 1906 to 1,572,000 in 1914. The conditions were being laid down for the great electoral leap forward which the Labour Party was to achieve during the early 1920s.

1) *The Labour Representation Committee and the parliamentary elections, 1900*
(Labour Party Archive, Walworth Road, London and reprinted in *Among Our Souvenirs*)

LABOUR REPRESENTATION AND THE ELECTIONS

The Elections which are just over have not been regarded with much satisfaction by Progressive politicians, but the Labour Representation Committee desires to bring before your notice the remarkable success which has met those candidates who have stood in harmony with the resolutions passed by the Conference of Labour Representation called in London last February by the Parliamentary Committee of the Trade Union Congress. Those resolutions declared in favour of uniting the Labour movement politically, not merely as a wing of any one of the existing parties, but as an expression of the necessity which has now arisen for Trade Unionists and others working for the emancipation of Labour, to adopt political methods in order to assist their other efforts.

Although there have been Labour members returned by various constituencies, and although individual Unions, as, for example, the Miners, have been directly represented in Parliament, there has been no united Labour movement in the country, advocating systematically the political claims and ideals which naturally supplement the economic claims and ideals of the working class and Trade Union organisations. There have been men, but there has been no movement.

The Labour Representation Committee was launched to impart unity and coherence to Labour politics, and to gather together the disconnected efforts of men and societies. Unfortunately, when only eight months old it had to face a General Election. The dissolution in September found the Committee with a membership of 312,000 (which has since increased to 350,000). Numbers of societies were still considering the question of affiliation, and several others were actually balloting their members on the subject. It had been impossible for the Committee to organise and consolidate the membership it had won. It had no power to recommend candidates, except those belonging to or promoted by affiliated societies, and its list was in consequence incomplete. It will be recognised that such conditions, together with the specially adverse state of public opinion which led to the defeat of four sitting Labour members and prevented another retaining a seat formerly held by a Liberal, told heavily against the chances of the Committee's candidates.

And yet, the Labour Representation Committee's list, despite several three-cornered contests, fared better than the average. Two members of the Committee actually won seats for Labour [the only victories which Labour gained at the election], and, in every case but one, where comparison with 1895 is possible, its candidates improved their polls. The votes polled were 62,698 out of a total of 177,000. In ten cases the local organisations responsible for the Committee's candidates were strong enough to keep one of the ordinary parties out of the contest; in the other five constituencies they had to fight both parties. This favourable result is due, in no small measure, to the existence of the Committee, and its manifesto to the electors in the constituencies where its candidates were running, was signed by representatives of all sections of the Labour movement. This is a happy augury for the future. 330,000 of these manifestoes were supplied gratis to the Committee's candidates. [. . .]

Issued on behalf of the Committee
J. RAMSAY MACDONALD
Hon. Secretary.

3, LINCOLN'S INN FIELDS, LONDON, W.C.
30th November, 1900

2) *The Taff Vale Case and its impact upon the Labour Representation, 1901 MacDonald's appeal to the trade unions on behalf of the LRC*
(*Echo*, 25 July 1901)
Trade unionism is being assailed, not by what the law says of it, but by what judges think the law ought to say of it. . . That being so, it becomes necessary for the unions to place men in the House of Commons, to challenge the decisions which I have no doubt will follow this.

3) *Letter from J. Bruce Glasier to his sister*
(Glasier Papers, Liverpool University Library, 1902/2)

Chapel-en-le Frith
via Stockport
26 March 1902

Dear Lizzie,

The fight [Wakefield by-election] is over and the battle lost but the defeat is to us almost as much a victory as a success would have been. At any rate we were never so merry after defeat as after this one. We feel that we have opened up a new avenue of political support in the future. The failure of the official Liberal set to run a candidate of their own, their recommendation of abstention, & then voting Tory, together with the revolt of the young Liberals and also the old radical to our side is a fine achievement.

Snowden fought superbly. His speaking was simply marvellous, and the whole campaign was without a hitch.

We are quote in glee about it. Then money, too, has come in abundantly – although there is no truth in the statement that we received £250 from Cadbury.

Bruce

4) *The aim and objectives of the Labour Representation Committee, as amended at the Newcastle Conference, February, 1903*
(Many Labour Representation Committee pamphlets)

I

The Labour Representation Committee is a Federation of Trade Unions, Trades Councils, the Independent Labour Party, and the Fabian Society. Co-operative Societies are also eligible for membership.

II

To secure, by united action, the election to Parliament of candidates promoted in the first instance, by an Affiliated Society or Societies in the constituency, who undertake to form or join a distinct group in Parliament, with its own whips and its own policy on Labour questions, to abstain strictly from identifying themselves with or promoting the interests of any section of the Liberal or Conservative parties, and not to oppose any other candidate recognised by this Committee. All such candidates shall pledge themselves to accept this Constitution, to abide by the decisions of the Group in carrying out the aims of this Constitution, or resign, and to appear before their constituencies under the title of Labour candidate only.

5) *Labour Representative Committee: Why We Are Independent* (Labour Representation Leaflets – No. 2)

WHY WE ARE INDEPENDENT

The Labour Representation Committee has decided that it must be an independent factor in politics, and it has been much criticised in consequence.

Let us quote the famous Newcastle resolution, and then explain why it was passed.

THE NEWCASTLE RESOLUTION

In view of the fact that the L.R.C. is recruiting adherents from all outside political forces, and also, taking into consideration the basis upon which the Committee was inaugurated, this Conference regards it as being absolutely necessary that the members of the E.C., Members of Parliament, and candidates run under the auspices of the Committee should strictly abstain from identifying themselves with or promoting the interests of any section of the Liberal or Conservative parties, inasmuch as if we are to secure the social and economic requirements of the industrial classes, Labour representatives in and out of Parliament will have to shape their own policy and act upon it regardless of other sections in the political world; and that the E.C. report to the affiliated associations or bodies any such official acting contrary to the spirit of the constitution as hereby amended.

Such is the resolution carried at Newcastle, by a vote of 659,000 against one of 154,000. This was the only possible decision, and the reason is apparent to anyone who understands the present position of the Labour movement.

THIS IS A NEW MOVEMENT

It originated in the desire of the workers for a party that really understands and is prepared to deal with their grievances, and has grown to its present strength by the systematic attacks in the Press and the Law Courts upon combined Labour and its funds. It is the workers' reply to the aggressive action of Federated Masters and Trusts.

But upon this conflict between Capital and Labour neither a Liberal nor a Conservative Ministry can be trusted to stand by the workers. The nation is called upon to settle economic and industrial difficulties for which neither of the old political parties offers any definite or satisfactory solution. Would it not, therefore, be futile to commit this new movement to parties which neither understand nor sympathise with its aims?

TRADE UNIONISM AND PARTY POLITICS

Consider also the composition of the Labour Representation Committee. The resolution of the Trades Union Congress which brought the Committee into existence, called for co-operation between the Trade Unionists, the Socialists, and the Co-operators. The movement is, therefore, not merely Trade Unionist, Socialist, or Co-operative, but one in which these three sections can work side by side for common aims and objects. [. . .]

THE WISDOM OF INDEPENDENCE

The only way to unite the democracy is to begin afresh, make a new appeal, raise a new issue, declare for a new political combination. [. . .]

WE ARE INDEPENDENT, THEN

Because we must unite the democracy;
Because we must have the support of all sections of the Labour movement;
Because if we are Liberal or Conservative, the Trade Union movement cannot unitedly support us;
Because this policy has already secured the support of about 1,000,000 Trade Unionists;
Because we raise new economic and industrial issues, upon which the old political parties speak with an uncertain and hesitating voice;
Because we must be free in Parliament to lay down our Labour policy

and adopt the most effective means for vindicating the rights of Labour and improving the social conditions of the people.

April, 1903   ISSUED ON BEHALF OF THE COMMITTEE,

J. RAMSAY MacDONALD, Secretary

6) *The Liberal–Labour Electoral Pact of 1903*

[In August 1903, Ramsay MacDonald and Herbert Gladstone secretly concluded the Liberal–Labour pact whereby the Labour Representation Committee would be allowed straight runs against the Conservatives in up to 30 seats without Liberal opponents, or in conjunction with Liberals in two-member constituencies, in return for reciprocal arrangements for Liberal candidates. The MacDonald papers are bereft of any hint, much less hard information, on this arrangement. Nevertheless, there is ample evidence of the negotiations in the Gladstone papers.]

(i) *Jesse Herbert in a memorandum to Herbert Gladstone, summarizing MacDonald's views*

(Memorandum by Jesse Herbert dated 6 March 1903, Gladstone Papers, Add. MSS. 46025, ff. 127–36. Also quoted in F. Bealey, 'Negotiations between the Liberal Party and the Labour Representation Committee before the general election of 1906', *Bulletin of the Institute of Historical Research*, vol. 29/30, 1956/7, pp. 265–6; P. Adelman, *The Rise of the Labour Party*, pp.107–8; D. Marquand, *Ramsay MacDonald*, p.78)

> A determination of the course to be followed by the Liberal party is urgently needed, for to do nothing is to seem to reject the overtures of the L.R.C., who may be irretrievably committed to courses during delay which they would avoid if they anticipated future friendly relations.
>
> [. . .] The official recognition of a separate group unpledged to support of the Liberal party, a group which will harrass every Government and whose representatives in Parliament will probably decline the Liberal whip, is not lightly to be given. It would be a vital change in the organization of parties. But would it be other than the official recognition of a fact, indisputable, and clear to every individual politician? There is no difficulty experienced in giving official recognition to the League group which has wealth. Why should there be difficulty in giving official

recognition to the Labour group which has numbers? Neither asks for an official approval of its objects, but both seek the friendly concession by the party of liberty to run their candidates unhampered by the presence of official candidates.

Are the principles and objects of the L.R.C. such as to justify such a benevolent attitude? Will the success of the Liberal party at the polls be too dearly purchased at the price? Ought the Liberal party to prefer defeat rather than assist in any way to foster the growing power of the Labour Party?

These are questions the answers to which necessitate an excursus into a political discussion which it would be presumptuous of one to make. I am concerned with the electoral prospects of the party, and anxiously ask myself, 'What would be the gain and the loss to the party at the General Election, if a working arrangement were arrived at with the L.R.C.?' [. . .]

The L.R.C. can directly influence the votes of nearly a million men. They will have a fighting fund of £100,000. (This is a most significant new fact in the situation. Labour candidates have had hitherto to beg for financial help, and have fought with paltry and wholly insufficient funds.) Their members are mainly men who have hitherto voted with the Liberal Party. Should they be advised to vote against Liberal candidates, and (as they probably would) should they act as advised the Liberal party would suffer defeat not only in the constituencies where L.R.C. candidates fought, but in almost every borough, and in many of the Divisions of Lancashire and Yorkshire. This would be the inevitable result of unfriendly action towards the L.R.C. candidates. They would be defeated, but so also should we be defeated.

If there be good-fellowship between us and the L.R.C. the aspect of the future for both will be very bright and encouraging.

(ii) *The J.D. Macrae and J.R. MacDonald correspondence on the Leeds West constituency*

(Labour Party, Labour Representation Committee Correspondence, 28/216, 28/217, 28/218)

[Herbert Gladstone was MP for Leeds West, one of those seats which MacDonald had agreed would be left to the Liberals. But, towards the end of 1905, J.D. Macrae informed MacDonald that the local LRC was intending putting forward a candidate for this seat. MacDonald responded by suggesting that he had been promised that only one Leeds constituency would be contested by Labour. When Macrae responded by implying that Mac-Donald had come to a political arrangement with Gladstone, MacDonald replied with a highly emotional letter denouncing the accusation. In the event, the general election occurred before a Labour candidate could be arranged for Leeds West.]

a. *Ramsay MacDonald to J.D. Macrae, 6 December 1905*

[. . .] I expect my Committee will pass a very strong resolution against any further candidature being undertaken. We have a very heavy national responsibility upon our shoulders. When we recommended O'Grady's Society to allow him to go to Leeds it was on the understanding that only one candidate was to be run and we shall probably have to communicate with his Executive upon the present situation. What form this communication will take I do not know. Judging, however, from what I have heard, my Executive will even go to the length of publishing a condemnatory resolution in the newspapers. . .

b. *Macrae to MacDonald, 7 December 1905*

What is the matter with West Leeds? Dear me, national responsibility, only one candidate, condemnatory resolution in the newspaper, national movement has suffered, dissociating ourselves from such a policy. What a flutter in the dovecotes. What did you say? Chief Liberal Whip, how very rude, it really is too bad for you. Now do be good boys, remember the honour and dignity of the movement depend upon your conduct.

c. *MacDonald to Macrae, 8 December 1905*

Dear Macrae,

May I say with reference to your impertinent ending . . . when some of you have done and have gone through as many temptations to do otherwise we will take your reference to "Chief Liberal Whip" as being of some value. Meanwhile I shall be much obliged if you would continue to do your want and have at any rate the common courtesy to remember that your reckless charges only bring contempt upon yourself and not upon those against whom they are directed. I shall, of course, put your letter and its "private hint" before my Committee on the 14th.

7) *John Lister's criticism of the Alliance/Lib–Lab arrangement in the 1905/6 General Election*
(John Lister Collection, Calderdale Archives Department. SH/JN/B/60)

The Lost Party   Tom Halifax   *c.* 1906

Oh! Where can it be – the old ILP?
   The party of sinews and brawn?
Oh! Where is the muscle, that once used to tussle
   With foes in the days that are gone?

The days that have been – will their like ne'er be seen?
   When courage and candour stood tall
Ere we entered the ways – yes the policy ways
   And hearken to history's warning!
'Tis this – that to laike with the old yellow-shirted 'snake'
(alternative version – with Whig or with Liberal to jig)
   Is a spree you may rue in the morning.

Anything! Anything! just to get in –
Any tale! Any tale! so you may win –
All the false lying spirits unchain,
Barter your soul man, your voter to claim.

8) *The Labour electoral manifesto, 1906*
(Labour Party Archives, LRC material)
[This was a moderate programme, at a time when the Labour Party contained socialists though it was not overtly a socialist party.]
To the Electors –

This election is to decide whether or not Labour is to be fairly represented in Parliament.

The House of Commons is supposed to be the people's House, and yet the people are not there.

Landlords, employers, lawyers, brewers, and financiers are there in force. Why not Labour?

The Trade Unions ask the same liberty as capital enjoys. They are refused.

The aged poor are neglected.

The slums remain; overcrowding continues, whilst the land goes to waste.

Shopkeepers and traders are overburdened with rates and taxation, whilst the increasing land values, which should relieve the ratepayers, go to the people who have not earned them.

Wars are fought to make the rich richer, and underfed school children are still neglected.

Chinese Labour is defended because it enriches the mine owners.

The unemployed ask for work, the Government gave them a worthless Act, and now, when you are beginning to understand the cause of your poverty, the red herring of Protection is drawn across your path.

Protection, as experience shows, is no remedy for poverty and unemployment. It serves to keep you from dealing with the land, housing, old age, and other social problems!

You have it in your power to see that Parliament carries out your wishes. The Labour Representation Executive appeals to you in the name of a million Trade Unionists...

9) *Victor Grayson and the Socialist Movement*
[In 1906, Victor Grayson was elected to be the Socialist candidate for Colne Valley. Despite the hostility of Ramsay MacDonald, who had secretly agreed that Colne Valley would be left to the Liberals in the Lib–Lab pact, Grayson stood and was returned for Colne Valley in the parliamentary by-election of July, 1907. He was in Parliament for three years, where he was at odds with his ILP and Labour Party colleagues. Just before the First World War he withdrew from active Labour politics and, after the war, disappeared from public view under suspicious circumstances which has led to speculation that he was murdered or was in the payment of the secret service.]
(i)   *Victor Grayson's Election Appeal, 1907*
(W. Thompson, *Victor Grayson MP*)

To the Electors in the Colne Valley. I am appealing to you as one of your own class. I want emancipation from the wage-slavery of Capitalism.

I do not believe that we are divinely destined to be drudges. Through the centuries we have been the serfs of an arrogant aristocracy.

We have toiled in the factories and workshops to grind profits with which to glut the greedy man of the Capitalist class.

Their children have been fed upon the fat of the land.

Our children have been neglected and handicapped in the struggle for existence.

We have served the classes and we have remained a mob.

The time for our emancipation has come.

We must break the rule of the rich and take our destinies into our hands.

Let charity begin with our children.

Workers who respect their wives, who love their children, and who long for a fuller life for all, a vote for the Landowner or Capitalist is treachery to your class.

To give your child a better chance than you have had, think carefully ere you make your cross.

The other classes have had their day. It is our turn now! Albert Victor Grayson.

(ii)   *Victor Grayson's victory speech*
(W. Thompson, *Victor Grayson, MP*)

The very first joy that comes to my mind is this, that this epoch making victory has been won for pure revolutionary Socialism. We have not trimmed our sails to get a half-hearted vote. We have proclaimed our Socialism on every platform. . . I have been returned through the work, the devotion, the love, the idealism of the people of the Colne Valley, and being returned I shall feel that my duty is to be the old men and women's member, the young men and women's member, the starving child's member, the one who will stand above all things for human legislation first. . . You have voted, you have worked for Socialism: you have voted, you have worked for the means of life to be the property of the whole class instead of a few small classes. We stand for equality, human equality, sexual equality – for the abolition of sex ties. . . It is a splendid victory, comrades.

(iii) *Grayson's socialist ideals*
(V. Grayson, *The Destiny of the Mob*)

We who are Socialists are not pessimistic of the results. We feel we can trust the instincts that have been chastened through ages of oppression and suffering. Enlightened democracy surely will not be brutal to itself. The final Revolution, on the threshold of which we are now standing, will be different from the Revolutions of the past. They were Revolutions of class against class, for the acquisition of personal or political power. This will be a Social Revolution to achieve the right to live. It is only another stage in the cycle of evolution. [. . .]

SOCIALISM INEVITABLE

[. . .] The stale commonplaces of individualism can no longer hold and inspire. Youth is cutting its moorings and embarking with a live spirit of hope on this new quest for human salvation. Men and women are growing sick of the old codes and systems. A new hope for humanity has been kindled in their hearts. Life is not for private profit, nor the soul for a lifeless bargain. The world may be rejuvenated. The filthy factory smirking the lovely sky and fouling the sparkling stream will be replaced by the beautiful workshop, where the work is worth doing, and blesses the individual who does it.

10) *The Right to Work Manifesto*
(Right to Work National Council, *The Right to Work Manifesto.* Copies in the Labour Party Archives)
Fellow Citizens,

Unemployment is still on the increase. No section of the workers are exempt. The official figures – in September – show that very nearly 9 per cent of the skilled workers of the country are workless. These figures . . . do not include . . . the unorganised and unskilled . . .

Parliament will meet in October. Before that time, every member must be made to understand by his constituents that his first duty at the opening of the Session is to insist upon the immediate amendment of the Unemployed Workmen Act, 1905. I` is a mockery and a delusion for those who are suffering, and ar   ccuse for inaction by politicians. [. . .]

11) *Ben Tillett's criticism of the Labour Party, 1908*
(Ben Tillett, *Is the Parliamentary Labour Party a failure?*)
The House of Commons and the country, which respected and feared

the Labour Party, are now fast approaching a condition of contempt towards its Parliamentary representatives.

The lion has no teeth or claws, and is losing his growl, too; the temperance section being softly feline in their purring to Ministers and their patronage. Those of the Party, who, out of a sense of loyalty to others, refrain from protest, indicate more patience than courage in their attitude ...

Labour is robbed of the wealth and means of life created by the genius of toil; the exploiters are on trial for their malefactions; the charge is that capitalist ownership of the land and material wealth is the cause of poverty. When that has been sufficiently explained and taught the people, there will be ample time for side issues, after the real work is done. I do not hesitate to describe the conduct of these blind leaders as nothing short of betrayal especially with the fact in view that they have displayed great activity for temperance reform than for Labour interests. Of all the farces, these same Labour-Temperance advocates knew the Bill would never pass the House of Lords; if not, they are not merely innocent but they are ignorant of their business, and cannot see an inch before their noses. Every Labour man knew the attitude of the Lords; all the Liberals did, for the game was played with the cards on the table. What a mockery it was, and merely a waste of time. While Shackleton took the chair for Winston Churchill, thousands of textile workers were suffering starvation through unemployment; his ability and energy could have been well used in Stevenson Square, in Manchester, instead of mouthing platitudes and piffle in Liberal meetings. The worst of the winter is coming on, time thrown away will never be recovered, and thousands will perish for want of bread. A great many of the victims to destitution will be in their graves before the Liberal Government will have approached the subject of unemployment, which they will sandwich between abolition of the House of Lords and Welsh Disestablishment. The temperance section, in particular, will be seizing on the other 'red-herrings', and the winter will have passed, and these unctious weaklings will go on prattling their nonsense, while thousands are dying of starvation. Some of these lives might have been saved to the country, the misery consequent to foodless condition of life averted. Blessed valuable months have been lost; the Labour movement must not tolerate the further betrayal of interests with agitations about the

House of Lords, or Welsh Disestablishment.

12) *The Osborne Judgement, 1909*

[The Osborne Judgement of 1909 made illegal the political levy – trade union contributions to the Labour Party – and led to a loss of income to the party and a loss of membership. Trade union members were expected to contract in to such a scheme after the judgement, and many did not do so.]

(i) *How the Osborne Judgement dooms Trade Unionism*
(Labour Party, *Labour Party Leaflet, no. 49*)

A few Judges have decided that Trade Unions must not defend their members and advance their interests by political means.

Landlords,
Railway Directors,
Brewers,   } can go to the House of Commons
Rich men generally,

But Labour is forbidden by the Judges to adopt the only means by which working men can get there.

The Rich can draw *Cheques for Thousands of Pounds* to finance their political friends. That is all right!

Both political parties *sell honours* to their wealthy followers, and thus maintain secret political funds. That is all right!

People who, under Tariff Reform, will be better able than now to *become rich at the Nation's expense*, keep the coffers of the Tariff Reform League full. That is all right!

But when *combined Labour tries to help the poor* by the use of its combined funds – the only way the coppers can be made as effective as cheques – the Judges say '*That is illegal!*'

Thus there is still one law for the Rich, and another for the Poor

How can Trade Unions do their work with this power taken from them? Parliament has become the field upon which the great battles between capital and labour are to be fought. By using its political power, Trade Unionism has won the

Workmen's Compensation Act,
Factory and Mining Legislation,
Unemployed Workmen's Act,
Fair Wages in Government Contracts

and similar Working-class benefits.

They have secured freedom of combination, and they repelled the last attack made upon their liberties by the unjust Taff Vale Decision.

In the future are they to be, like a shorn Samson, at the mercy of the Philistines?

(ii) *MacDonald's attack upon the Liberal Government for failing to draw up a bill to reverse the Osborne Judgement*

(*Socialist Review*, September 1910)

[The Liberal Government's] attitude was tantamount to a declaration of war ... It is to stand supinely by whilst Trade Unionism is being imprisoned within such narrow bounds that it cannot meet with any success the attacks that are now being made upon it. This is a new factor in the situation, and it ought to influence the attitude of the Parliamentary Party.

(iii) *Recent Research*

(R. McKibbin, *The Evolution of the Labour Party, 1910–1924*)

Of the local party records that survive, virtually every one shows that the Judgement led to a steady fall in the affiliated membership and thus in revenue. Even the strongest parties, like Manchester and Leeds, were badly hit, while for tender flowers, like the Liverpool L.R.C., the Judgement was almost fatal. A surprisingly large number of the L.R.C.s collapsed completely or disaffiliated – how many cannot be discovered exactly – and the Judgement ensured that there was effectively no rise at all in the number of L.R.C.s or trades councils affiliated to the national Party between 1910 and 1913. Finally, it should be noted that the enjoining of unions under the Judgement made then determined to keep their levies to the Party artificially low when Party finances were reorganized in 1912.

13) *Party Organisation, 1911: MacDonald to the Labour Party parliamentary members*
(Labour Party Archives, and reprinted in *Among Our Souvenirs*)

The House of Commons,
S.W.
7 Feb., 1911

To the Members of the Labour Party
Dear Sir,

When you were good enough to elect me as your chairman I accepted the responsibility after a good deal of hesitation. I have been troubled in my own mind for sometime about three matters; –

1.   The foolish criticism passed upon us by our members in the country.

2.   The slackness of individual members in the House of Commons;

3.   The lack of party cohesion and of a general enthusiastic backing of each individual member, either when he is attacked or is attacking, in the House of Commons.

I feel quite sure that, unless we can put an end to these things, our Party's usefulness will be jeopardized.

I therefore appeal to you to co-operate in securing and keeping for the Party the position which is its due, and to that end I make the following observations:–

a. *Loyalty in the House.*

[. . .] A demonstration of the virile unity of a party is just as important as the speeches of its members. [. . .]

f. *Speaking on Platforms,* &c.

May I also draw your attention to the importance of your loyalty standing by Party decisions when you speak, give interviews etc. Sometimes the Party finds itself pledged beforehand on important matters of policy, and when negotiations are on foot, an awkward speech by a Member may involve your Officers in serious entanglements. This is a large and difficult problem, but the Rule which should be adopted is that Party meetings are the place to discuss differences. [. . .]

THE FIRST WORLD
WAR, 1914–1918

The First World War helped to transform the position of the British Labour Party. It divided the Liberal Party, as Asquith came into conflict with David Lloyd George over the conduct of the War. There is no doubt that the Labour Party filled the vacuum left by the fragmentation of the Liberal Party, although its political growth may well have occurred even without the War. The War also saw the Labour Party join with the Coalition Government, thus enhancing its claims to the status of a potential party of government. Trade union membership, the basis of Labour's growth, also increased from about four million to more than six million during the war years. It was during the War that the Labour Party introduced a new constitution which emphasised its commitment to socialism (4).

Nevertheless, the War divided the Labour Party as it did the Liberals. Although the Labour leaders had declared their opposition in August 1914, they were quickly sucked into the war effort, and the Party joined the Coalition Government in May 1915. The majority of trade unionists were also pro-war, although their support became less resolute after the introduction of military conscription in 1916. However, some socialists could not commit themselves to Labour's pro-war stance. Indeed, Ramsay MacDonald gave up his leading position in the Labour Party, although he gradually drifted back into the party in 1917 and 1918. Yet the most determined opposition came from the Independent Labour Party. Although even members of the ILP were divided between pro-war and anti-war attitudes, Philip Snowden ensured that the ILP's official policy remained opposed to the War. Snowden was not a pacifist but felt that the War was unnecessary and, in building up the National Debt, threatened to slow down the pace of progress towards socialism.

Snowden's concern was to push for peace as quickly as possible and he made his 'Plea for Peace' in the House of Commons in 1916 (1), following on from the suggestion of President Wilson that the various combatants should declare their terms of peace. By 1917, when the Peace Movement was well under way, the Labour Party also declared its terms for a future lasting peace (3). The gist of its statement was that genuine and continuing peace could only be secured if it was established between democratic nations which were not intent upon imperial aggrandisement and reparations. It also committed itself to a League of Nations to help to maintain the peace in the post-war world (3).

The Labour Party did not see the achievement of its objectives, and Philip Snowden's Peace Campaign failed despite the sterling efforts he made (2). Yet during the First World War a relatively disunited Labour Party emerged into a confident and assertive party with a new constitution, an improved organisation, and a commitment to the collective ownership of the means of production (4). It had defined its position in such a way that it could no longer be regarded as the 'tail of the Liberal Party'. By the end of the War it had broken the traditional mould of two-party politics and was on course to be a party of government.

1) *Philip Snowden's 'Plea for Peace' in the House of Commons, 1916* (P. Snowden, *A Plea for Peace*)
The outstanding lesson of this War is that militarism stands discredited. It is now proved to be a futile method of serving aggressive designs. No great modern nation can conquer or be conquered, and that fact has a most vital relation to the conditions of peace. If it now be the fact that military power is useless for the purpose of aggrandisement and aggression, then these conditions and the future relations of Europe must be governed by that fact. An inconclusive ending to this War, in the sense that all the belligerent Powers realise the futility of military power would be the surest guarantee against a repetition of war ...

OUR GOVERNMENT'S RESPONSIBILITY

I submit that the facts I have adduced prove that there is reasonable ground for believing that the present is a favourable opportunity for holding out the hand of negotiation. I am sure that such an effort coming from this Government, speaking with all the authority that this Government could do, would be heartily welcomed, and it would find a hearty response from the sorely striken people of other countries, and would be regarded by German Socialists as an encouragement to them to increase their efforts to secure a peace as I am quite sure all parties might regard as an honourable and satisfactory end of this War. I am fully aware of the difficulty, but I was especially gratified by the tone and terms of a reply to a question which I addressed to the Prime Minister last December, in which he said the Allied Governments would be willing to consider any serious proposals for peace which might come from belligerent or neutral countries.

ONE STEP FURTHER

The Prime Minister only needs to go one step further. He can give encouragement to offers of peace. . . There are many channels open to the Government through which negotiations may be opened up, and we have the right to demand that the Government shall state in much more definite and precise language the terms upon which they would be willing to consider peace.

2) *Philip Snowden, 'War or Peace', 13 February 1918*
(P. Snowden, *War or Peace*)
The Military situation today is no more hopeful than it was twelve months ago. If we go another twelve months it will be less hopeful than it is today. [. . .] During the last twelve months, for no military advantage whatever, we have sacrificed in killed and wounded, according to the returns of the War Office, a million men . . . I am looking for the conclusion of this way by a union of the democracies of all belligerent nations. They have learned that lesson in common affliction and although one can hardly say that any good which may result from this war would be anything of a compensation for the stupendous evil which it has created, still it would be something if, as a result of this war, we had for ever a sweeping away of the power of those who have misused their powers in the past and have used them, not for the good of the people, but in order to satisfy their own Imperialist and selfish aims.

3) *Statement of the War Aims of the Labour Party, 1917*
(Labour Party Archives, London. Also in ed. P. Stansky, *The Left and War: The British Labour Party and World War I*)
As adopted at a joint conference of the societies affiliated with the British Trades Union Congress and the British Labour Party at Central Hall, Westminster, on December 28, 1917.

1. *The War*
The British Labour movement sees no reason to depart from the declaration unanimously agreed to at the Conference of the Socialist and Labour Parties of the Allied Nations on February 14, 1915, and it reaffirms that declaration. Whatever may have been the causes of the outbreak of war, it is clear that the peoples of Europe, who are necessarily the chief sufferers from its horrors, had themselves no hand in it. Their common interest is now so to conduct the terrible struggle in which they find themselves engaged as to bring it, as soon as may be possible, to an issue in a secure and lasting peace for the world.

2. *Making the world safe for democracy*
Whatever may have been the causes for which the war was begun, the fundamental purpose of the British Labour movement in supporting the continuance of the struggle is that the world may henceforth be made safe for democracy.

Of all the war aims, none is so important to the people of the world as that there shall be henceforth on earth no more war. Whoever triumphs, the people will have lost unless some effective method of preventing war can be found.

As means to this end, the British Labour movement relies very largely upon the complete democratisation of all countries; on the frank abandonment of every form of Imperialism; on the suppression of secret diplomacy, and on the placing of foreign policy, just as much as home policy, under the control of popularly elected Legislatures; on the absolute responsibility of the Foreign Minister of each country to its Legislature; on such concerted action as may be possible for the universal abolition of compulsory military service in all countries, the common limitation of the costly armaments by which all people are burdened, and the entire abolition of profit-making armaments firms, whose pecuniary interest lies always in war scares and rivalry in preparation for war.

But it demands, in addition, that it should be an essential part of the treaty of peace itself that there should be forthwith established a Supernational Authority, or League of Nations, which should not only be adhered to by all the present belligerents, but which every other independent sovereign state in the world should be pressed to join; the immediate establishment of such League of Nations not only of an International High Court for the settlement of all disputes between states that are of justifiable nature, but also of appropriate machinery for prompt and effective mediation between states at issue that are not justifiable; the formation of an International Legislature, in which the representatives of every civilised state would have their allotted share; the gradual development, as far as may prove to be possible, of international legislation agreed to by and definitely binding upon the several states, and for a solemn agreement and pledge by all states that every issue between any two or more of them shall be submitted for settlement as aforesaid, and that they will all make common cause against any state which fails to adhere to this agreement.

3. *Territorial adjustments*

The British Labour movement has no sympathy with the attempts made, now in this quarter and now in that, to convert this war into a war of conquest, whether what is sought to be acquired by force is territory or wealth, nor should the struggle be prolonged for a single day, once the conditions of a permanent peace can be secured, merely for the sake of extending the boundaries of any state.

But it is impossible to ignore the fact that, not only restitution and reparation, but also certain territorial readjustments are required if a renewal of armaments and war is to be avoided. These readjustments must be such as can be arrived at by common agreement on the general principle of allowing all people to settle their own destinies, and for the purpose of removing any obvious cause of future international conflict.

4) *The Labour Party Constitution, 1918*
(Labour Party Archives, London)
  1. *Name*
The Labour Party
  2. *Membership*
The Labour Party shall consist of all its affiliated organisations, together with those men and women who are individual members of a Local Labour Party and who subscribe to the Constitution and Programme of the Party.
  3. *Party Objects*
National
(a) To organise and maintain in Parliament and in the country a Political Labour Party, and to ensure the establishment of a Local Labour Party in every County Constituency and every Parliamentary Borough with suitable divisional organisation in the separate constituencies of Divided Boroughs;
(b) To co-operate with the Parliamentary Committee of the Trade Union Congress, or other Kindred Organisations, in joint political or other action in harmony with the Party Constitution and Standing Orders;
(c) To give effect as far as may be practicable to the principles from time to time approved by the Party Conference;
(d) To secure for producers by hand or by brain the full fruits of their industry, and the most equitable distribution thereof that may be possible, upon the basis of the common ownership of the means of production and the best obtainable system of popular administration and control of each industry or service;
(e) Generally to promote the Political, Social, and Economic Emancipation of the People, and more particularly of those who depend directly upon their own exertions by hand or by brain for the means of life.

LABOUR'S GROWTH, 1918–1929

In 1918 the Labour Party was still a relatively small body with only 63 MPs in the House of Commons. In 1929 it was the largest parliamentary party in the nation, with 288 MPs, though not enough to form a majority Labour government. During the intervening years it had completely transformed its political position. But why had this occurred? Christopher Howard, in an article entitled 'Expectation born to death: local Labour party expansion in the 1920s', in *Working Class in Modern British History: Essays in Honour of Henry Pelling* has questioned the effectiveness of Labour's organisation and suggested that the Labour Party was lucky to grow as it did. He argues that 'The image of a vibrant expanding new party was an illusion. Labour was fortunate that its opponents were deceived.' And again, 'Widespread electoral success bore little resemblance to restricted party membership. . .' Yet it is precisely this perceived gap between organisation and performance which is intriguing. If it did occur, it says something about the strength of working-class support for Labour and the strength of class politics. However, it is quite clear that whilst Labour's working-class support was extremely high in the 1920s the Party's organisation was vibrant, active and effective, in many areas of the country.

The Labour Party's national organisation was thoroughly improved between 1918 and 1924 (1) through the extension of its constituency organisation, its newspaper propaganda and the active organisation of women. The only blackspot was the lamentably low number of party agents it employed. The Independent Labour Party, still affiliated to the Labour Party until 1932, was also intent upon rebuilding its organisation and membership, which had declined during the War, and the demand for change was led by Philip Snowden (2, 3, 4, 5) – despite his concern about the rising level of Bolshevik sympathy within the ILP.

As the political support for Labour increased it became more important than ever that it should develop and publicise its policies. Yet despite its advocacy of state socialism, it always presented itself as a responsible party, moderate and balanced in its approach and committed to gradual change. This was most effectively demonstrated in its economic policies which can best be traced through the writings and speeches of Philip Snowden. His economic policies were most orthodox – believing in free trade, the balancing of the budget, and the repayment of the National Debt through the Sinking Fund – views which are neatly presented, in part, in the *Big Business Budget* and *The Housewife's Budget* (6, i, ii). Snowden believed that sound finance, as he called his views, was the essential precursor of socialism.

Labour's propensity for moderation was amply demonstrated when it took office, for the first time, in January 1924. Stanley Baldwin, the Conservative Prime Minister, had fought the December 1923 General Election on the issue of protection. Although the Conservative Party was returned as the largest parliamentary party it was clear that the free trade parties, Labour and the Liberals, had an overall majority in Parliament. As a result, Baldwin stood down in favour of the Labour Party, the largest of the two free trade parties. Although supported by the Liberals, the Labour government lasted less than ten months. It was remarkably moderate (7, i), determined to prove itself as a responsible party of government, but, in the end, MacDonald's attempt to open up trading and diplomatic relations with the Soviet Union, and the mishandling of the Campbell case whereby the Attorney General was going to prosecute Campbell for incitement to mutiny but eventually decided not to go ahead, paved the way for Liberal amendments to the Russian treaties and a Conservative censure of Labour's handling of the Campbell case (7, ii). Defeated in Parliament, MacDonald offered the resignation of his government to the King and called a general election. This was marked by the 'Red Letter Scare', the printing of the Zinoviev letter indicating the intention of the Russians to use the Labour Party to extend Leninist ideas (8). This might well have been a forgery but it seems doubtful whether it did much damage to the Labour Party's political performance.

For the next five years Labour continued its steady progress, during which there were perhaps only two significant developments. The first was the General Strike of 1926, a nine-day strike organised by the Trades Union Congress in support of the locked-out miners. During this dispute, the Party was criticised for not being more involved in the direction of the dispute but reminded its critics that the TUC, not the Labour Party, 'are the custodians of the industrial side of the matter' (9, i, ii). Nevertheless, the defeat of the General Strike seems to have increased the commitment of trade unions towards supporting political action during the late 1920s and united the two sides of the movement more firmly than before.

The second development was the increasing frustration with MacDonald. In opposition, between 1924 and 1929, he had made remarkably little showing and it was suggested that he was becoming distant from his colleagues. There were rumours, in 1926 and 1927, that he might be replaced by Philip Snowden and Arthur Henderson. These never came to fruition but the tensions between the leading figures in the Party were most obviously evident in the candid letter which Snowden wrote to MacDonald in October 1927 (10). But Snowden's comments were merely a reflection of the frustrations which had been developing towards MacDonald for a number of years. Similar strains were evident in MacDonald's relations with the Independent Labour Party. The *Bradford Pioneer*, 12 March 1926, likened MacDonald's relationship with the ILP to a lovers' quarrel:

MacDonald is an amazing personality: rarely has a democratic leader found such difficulty in opening his real mind to his party, and for decades now the story of his relation to his followers has been one of a lovers' quarrel, tiffs followed by happy reconciliation. He is always estranging us, and then just when we begin to wonder if the honeymoon is over, winning us back again.

Just over three years later, in May 1929, a new honeymoon began when the Labour Party was returned to office as the largest parliamentary party in British politics, though without an overall majority. Two and a quarter years later the estrangement became permanent with

MacDonald's 'betrayal', the end of the second Labour Government and the formation of the National Government.

1) *The Re-organisation of the Labour Party, 1918–1924*

(i)   *Number of Affiliated Divisional Labour Parties and Trades Councils*
(R. McKibbin, *The Evolution of the Labour Party*, p.137)

Jan. 1918	215	1921	498
June 1918	397	1922	527
1919	400	1923	573
1920	433	1924	626

(ii)   (*Leeds Weekly Citizen*, 5 November 1918)
It would be a disaster if the Coalition Association Ltd were allowed to control the reconstruction period without a most powerful opposition.

(iii)   *Newspaper Propaganda*
(*Bradford Pioneer*, 7 March 1919)
Don't destroy this paper. Lend it. Become a Pioneer Pusher. Persuade your friends and workmates to order it. If YOU can sell a few in your workshop let us know and we will send them along. New readers means the extension of Labour's influence in world politics. 'Nuff said'. Get busy.

(iv)   *Women's Organisations*
(The Archive of the British Labour Party, National Executive Committee, Minutes, report submitted 23 June 1919)
Attention was given to Lancashire and Cheshire, the West Riding of Yorkshire, and the Black Country. [...] Advisory Councils are now in the process of formation in the West Riding of Yorkshire and the Black Country.

(v)   *Number of Agents and Supplementary Agents connected with the Labour Party*
(R. McKibbin, *The Evolution of the Labour Party 1910–1924*, p.143)

Year	Agents	Supplementary Agents
1920	112	24
1921	127	22
1922	133	23
1923	111	26
1924	113	36

2) *The rebuilding of the Independent Labour Party: Part of a letter from Philip Snowden to J. Bruce Glasier, revealing Snowden's enthusiasm for the revival of the ILP*
(Glasier Papers, 1/1919/101)

2 February 1919

My dear Bruce,
 [. . .] For the last fortnight my mind day and night has been full of the *Leader*. I have scores of brilliant ideas for making it the biggest, brightest, best, most useful, most popular paper in the world. I feel so keenly about this that I would like to take on the editorship with Mrs. Glasier as partner. I could live to make it a success as I have never lived for a purpose before. [. . .]

Philip Snowden

3) *Part of a letter from Philip Snowden to Mrs Bruce Glasier, defending state intervention and advocating action to revive the Independent Labour Party after the First World War*
(Glasier Papers, 1/1919/100)

 It is the business of the profiteers to work this charge of Bureaucracy in their interest. They want to discredit State enterprise. I believe that things have been bad, but not so bad as our enemies are endeavouring to make out. For instance, last week at the Jordans, Willie Leach was speaking most highly about the ability and business capacity of the Government officials who are controlling the wool supply and the contracts for the manufacture of cloth. We must be careful not to allow ourselves to be used by the profiteers in their attacks on State management. It is for us to steer the middle course and point out dangers and abuses of Bureaucracy where they exist and to show these are not intents of state control, but that the abuses are due to the abuses of democratic supervision. [. . .]

 We had a most wonderful time at Jordans, the most useful conference I think I have ever attended. [. . .] The need for an energetic forward movement by pamphlets and books was reached and schemes were suggested for meeting the need. I want to see the Labour Press with its great resources turned into a munition factory for our Socialist propaganda. I am quite willing to give a good deal of my time to this work. We want leaflets and we want pamphlets, and we

projected last week, a series of Socialist books to sell at 1/-. With your
... knowledge of what the readers of the *Labour Leader* are wanting
you could help us with suggestions ...

Philip Snowden

4) *Letter from J. Bruce Glasier to Philip Snowden, April 1920, about the
impending National ILP Conference at which there was to be discussion
about the rival claims of the Second International and the Third International,
or Comintern*
(Glasier Papers, 1920/95)

2 April 1920

My dear Snowden,

   [...] I understand that one of the chief objects before the Conference will be the question of the rival claims of the Second and Third
International and I hear it said that there may be a split in the Party
over the question. Indeed I do not believe it. I cannot believe that the
I.L.P. is going to disrupt itself upon a matter which however important
it may seem in principle, presents such confused and contradictory
issues to equally earnest minds. [...]

   I had hoped that long ere now we should have been successful in
bringing about a re-assembly of the full International in which every
nation and section, voted in its Socialist constitution, whether majority
or minority, would have due representation, and in which the theme of
discussion would not be what was said and done in the past at all, but
what has to be said and done in the future. Only now when the
blinding flames, and the suffocating and maddening fumes of the war
are clearing away is it possible for the Socialist sections to see each
other fairly and consider weekly the great task of re-establishing
International Socialism, not with eyes of anger and vindication, but
of fellowship and faith. Let us not forget that the French Party
which today is overwhelmingly for meeting German Independents,
was all during the war almost unanimous against any assembly that
would include the German Socialists. No let us forget that when the
Russian Revolution was first achieved, the Workers and Soldiers'
Council which included all sections of the Russian democracy and
Menshavik as well as Bolshevik, and when as yet Lenin and Trotsky
were in exile, sent forth to the workers of Germany and Austria the

noblest message of International brotherhood ever issued across the frontiers of war.

Another word. I have the feeling which is, I believe, widely felt in the Party, that Trade Union politics and Trade Union affairs which have not assumed vast importance in the country, largely as a result of our Socialist propaganda, have recently had a tendency to overshadow and obscure our Socialist principles and aims. The Socialist movement is not simply a Trade Union, or for that matter an exclusively manual Labour movement – though it embraces, and must embrace, the organized workers and champion their causes. It is not merely a movement for obtaining better wages and workshop conditions for the workers, or even for abolishing the more glaring forms of poverty and capitalist monopoly. It is a movement for abolishing the causes of all industrial and social injustices and for the complete rebuilding [of] society on the basis of equality, co-operation and commonwealth.

Already in our own country and in the Revolution abroad, we perceive that it is only when we reach the stage of insurgent action by the Trade Unions and preliminary nationalization, that we encounter the real problems and tests of our principles and ourselves. It is then when we come face to face with the question: – are we really ready for democracy and socialism – for the methods of peace and reason rather than for resigning our selfish class fears and greed, and boldly entrusting our whole well being to the justice and good will of the community. For anything less than that is not socialism, just merely old-world striving for individual and class advantage. [. . .]

5) *Philip Snowden's reply to Bruce Glasier after the ILP Conference* (Glasier Papers, 1/1920/97)

9 April 1920

My Dear Bruce,
[. . .] My present feeling is one of relief rather than of satisfaction. I had feared that things might go worse. However, I think the danger point has been turned and events will make it less easy for the revolutionaries to carry on their activities within the Party in the future. The debate on the International was exceedingly good, the best, I think, I have heard in any of our Conferences. On the second day, every speaker who rose was against the Bolsheviks, and I had finally to

make an appeal either to bring the discussion to an open end or to get a speaker from the other side. It was unfortunate that so many of the delegates had come to the Conference pledged, or I am sure the vote for Moscow would have been much smaller than it was.

The new NAC seems strange to me, but when that feeling of reunion has passed probably we shall get along fairly well together. The loss of Benson is very serious. I believe he feels his severance very heavily. [. . .]

Philip Snowden

6) *Philip Snowden, Labour's Shadow Chancellor and first Chancellor of the Exchequer, expressing his commitment to economic orthodoxy by arguing the need for a reduction in National Debt in order to achieve economic growth*

(i) (P. Snowdon, *The Big Business Budget*)

. . . you cannot have a tax reduction on sound economic lines so long as the National Debt exists. [. . .]

One might think from the criticism made against the Labour Party during these debates that we are not in favour of lower taxation. We are in favour of lower taxation. What is the object of the proposal we put forward for a levy on capital, except to reduce the amount of debt and thus to reduce the amount of taxation necessary to pay the interest on the debt? The only difference, if we would only understand each other, between those who are demanding a reduction of taxation without regard to the debt and ourselves, is that we realise that you cannot reduce taxation till you have reduced the debt, and therefore the first thing is to reduce the debt in a thorough manner.

(ii) (P. Snowden, *The Housewife's Budget*, a verbatim report of the speech delivered by Snowden on the occasion of his first Budget speech on 29 April 1924)

Meanwhile, it is clear that we must take every opportunity and devote as much of our resources as possible to the redemption of Debt (Cheers). Some people seem to think that Debt reduction is something which confers no public advantage. I know a reduction of 1s in Income Tax is much more spectacular than paying off £50,000,000 of Debt. In the first case the relief is obvious, in the second, it is indirect, but none the less real, and in fact is more widespread and penetrating in its benefits.

Improvements in national credit in its turn regulate the rates at which money can be borrowed for industrial purposes.

7) *The First Labour Government, 1924*
(i) *MacDonald on the decision to take office, 1924*
(H. Hessell Tiltman, *James Ramsay MacDonald*, p.309)
[Emphasising that the Labour Party would be pragmatic in office, MacDonald stated that he wanted a Labour Government so that the life of the nation could be carried on.]
Nineteen-twenty-four is not the last in God's programme of creation. My friends, we will be dead and gone and forgotten and generation after generation, and there will still be the search for the Holy Grail by knights like Keir Hardie. The shield of love and the spear of justice will still be in the hands of good and upright men and women, and the ideal of a great future will still be in front of our people. I see no end, thank God, to these things ... I see my own skyline, but I am convinced that when my children or children's children get there there will be another skyline, another horizon, another dawning, another glorious beckoning from heaven itself.

(ii) *The Campbell Case and the Labour Cabinet, 1924*
[In an article which appeared in the *Worker's Weekly* John Campbell, the acting editor, called upon the British soldiers not to turn their guns upon the workers in the class war. The Labour Attorney decided to prosecute Campbell but the matter was finally dropped after much debate. This decision led to a motion of no-confidence against MacDonald and the Labour government, which, once carried, led to the October 1924 general election and the return of the Conservative Party under Stanley Baldwin.]

(a) *MacDonald's reaction*
(Quoted in D. Marquand, *Ramsay MacDonald*)
I sent for the Attorney General and the Public Prosecutor and gave them a bit of my mind... They replied that the whole matter could be dropped. I told them that, as they had begun, they had to go through with it. Later on I was informed that the editor was prepared to write a letter which would amount to an apology for what he had done. I agreed that, if he did that, the matter might be dropped.

(b) *Cabinet Meeting, 22 August 1924: minute of Tom Jones*
(Thomas Jones, *Whitehall Diary*, Vol. I, edited by K. Middlemass, p.287)

> [The Attorney General told the Cabinet that] inasmuch as it transpired that the person charged was only acting temporarily as editor and was prepared to write a letter to that effect steps could be taken not to press the prosecution in the circumstances against this particular offender, if the Cabinet so desired. [The Cabinet agreed:]
>
> > That no public prosecution of a political character should be undertaken without the prior sanction of the Cabinet being obtained.
> >
> > That in the particular case under review the course indicated by the Attorney-General should be adopted.

(c) *MacDonald, the Campbell Case and the House of Commons*
(Hansard (1924), vol. 177, col. 16)

> [The prosecution of Campbell was dropped on 13 August but towards the end of September 1924 it was raised in the House of Commons, after the summer recess, and the matter was discussed in the House on 30 September 1924. In answer to Sir Kingsley Wood's second private notice question, MacDonald answered in the following manner, which, to be polite, was stretching the truth.]
>
> I was not consulted regarding either the institution or the subsequent withdrawal of these proceedings. The first notice of the prosecution which came to my knowledge was in the Press. I never advised its withdrawal, but left the whole matter to the discretion of the Law Officers, where that discretion properly rests. I never received any intimation, not even a hint, that I should be asked to give evidence. [This was about giving evidence in favour of the defendent.] That also came to my attention when the falsehood appeared in the Press.

(d) *MacDonald's personal reflection upon the Campbell Case and a Liberal motion censuring the Labour Government's trade treaty with Russia*

(PRO, 30/69, 1753, MacDonald Diaries, 1910–1937, 1 October 1924)

> I am living in rare air tonight; the end is definitely in sight, & by a blunder of the Liberals my path has been cleared. The Tories are to censure us & it is expected that the Liberals will vote with them. Had the fall come upon the Attorney alone, & had his mistake been kept isolated from other issues, a dissolution would have been an awkward thing to ask for & an equally awkward thing to have justified to the country. Mr. Asquith's blunder is giving notice of a resolution to reject the Russian Treaty gives a general political significance to the vote of censure & bring the whole political forces into the battle. So I am unburdened tonight. . .

(e) *The end of the first Labour Government, 8 October 1924*

(PRO, 30/69, 1753, MacDonald Diaries, 1910–1937, 8 October 1924)

> 11.50 p.m. So the chapter ends after a great day when at the close we stood higher in the House of Commons than ever & when men going into the lobbies to defeat the Government showed no hilarity, but looked rather as though they were marching to their own destruction.

8) *The Zinoviev Letter, 1924*
(L. Chester, S. Fay and H. Young, *The Zinoviev Letter*)

Executive Committee   Very Secret
  Third Communist International

                                    To the Central Committee,
                                    British Communist Party

Presidium
  September 15th, 1924.
  Moscow
Dear Comrades,
  The time is approaching for the Parliament of England to consider

the Treaty concluded between the Governments of Great Britain and the S.S.S.R. for the purpose of ratification. . .

It is indispensable to stir up the masses of the British proletariat to bring into movement the army of unemployed proletarians whose position can be improved only after a loan has been granted to the S.S.S.R. . . . . A settlement of relations between the two countries will assist in the revolutionising of the international and British proletariat not less than a successful rising in any of the working districts of England, as the establishment of close contact between the British and Russian proletariat, the exchange of delegations and workers, etc., will make it possible for us to extend and develop the propaganda of ideas of Leninism in England and the Colonies. Armed warfare must be preceded by a struggle against the inclination to compromise which are embedded among the majority of British workmen, against the ideas of evolution and peaceful extermination of capitalism. Only then will it be possible to count upon complete success of an armed insurrection. . .

Form a directing operative head of the Military Section.

Do not put this off to a future moment, which may be pregnant with events and catch you unprepared.

Desiring you all success, both in organisation and in your struggle.

With Communist Greetings,

President of the Presidium of the I.K.K.I.

Members of the Presidium: McMANUS

Secretary: KUUSINEN

9) *The Labour Party and the General Strike, 1926*
(Labour Party, National Executive Committee, Minutes)
(i)   Minutes of E.C. . . . 28 April 1926 at 10.30 am
        Item 239   Mining Dispute
        Letters and resolutions were reported from the Chorley D.L.P. and other organisations, re the Mining Dispute.

        The Assistant Secretary reported that he had replied to these letters stating that propaganda literature has been published on the matter and suggesting that the miners' case could best be served by pushing the sale of literature and the 'Daily Herald'.

(ii) Organisation Committee, 21 June 1926
                      Report of Women's Work
                      19 April to 12 June

MINERS' WIVES AND CHILDREN RELIEF FUND

In addition to the above meetings of the Advisory Councils all the Councils in the Mining Districts or their officers have met to arrange for certain work to be done, which the Women's Committee for the Relief of Miners' Wives and Children asked them to undertake. They were asked to arrange for the distribution of foodstuffs and clothes for women and children, which would be sent by the National Committee, and also to be responsible for the distribution of a special fund which the Committees were collecting for expectant and nursing mothers and babies and invalid women and children.

The Women Organisers were asked to give the Advisory Councils all the help they could towards getting this scheme established and it is now running smoothly, the Advisory Councils, through the Women's Sections having got the machinery necessary in each mining community. [. . .]

GENERAL STRIKE PERIOD

During the General Strike period the women organisers assisted the local strike organisation in their areas. [. . .] Most of the organisers report increases of membership amongst the women in the Sections as a result of the Strike, and this is particularly so in the Mining Areas.

E.C. 1925–6
Minutes of E.C.   23 June 1926 at 10.30 am
281 [. . .] A letter was reported from the Manchester (Borough) Labour Party stating that the National Labour Party should give Local Parties a definite lead in dissipating the feeling of distrust and despair of political and industrial action resulting from the unsatisfactory conclusion of the general strike and suggesting the course the Executive should take to assist the miners.

RESOLVED 'That a reply be sent explaining the propaganda
    work in which the Party has been engaged, and stating that

the Trades Union Congress are the custodians of the industrial side of the matter.'

10) *Letter from Snowden to MacDonald criticising his increasing isolation from his political colleagues, 14 October 1927*
(PRO, 30/69 item 1753, MacDonald Diaries 1910–1937, letter at the front of the diaries)
My Dear MacDonald,

[. . .] Now that the Protocol has been buried at Geneva I do not see any reason why we cannot all unite upon an agreed policy for securing its fundamental aim of arbitration and disarmament.

[. . .] The second matter is this. And you must excuse me for writing quite plainly. I am expressing the feelings of all my colleagues who have talked with me on the subject. We are feeling that somehow – it is difficult to explain – we cannot get inside you. You seem to be protected by some impenetrable barrier. I called it aloofness in my last letter. It was not so in the old days of the N.A.C. It is difficult to express what I want to say. But perhaps I have said enough to give you an idea of what we feel.

Perhaps I may explain what I mean referring to an incident. [Snowden then gave a detailed example of a confusion of roles between Labour's leaders due to MacDonald's vagueness.]

RAMSAY MACDONALD AND THE 'BETRAYAL' OF THE SECOND LABOUR GOVERNMENT, 1929–1931

No British political leader this century has been more reviled than Ramsay MacDonald, Britain's first Labour Prime Minister. His decision to offer the resignation of the second Labour Government and to accept the King's commission to form a National Government during the financial crisis of August 1931 provoked much animus amongst many who knew him and believed in him, sustaining the view that he had planned to ditch the Labour Government for some time. It has long been an axiom of the Labour Party that MacDonald's actions in 1931 marked him as a traitor to the cause. A popular catch at the time rang

We'll hang Ramsay Mac on a sour apple tree,
We'll hang Snowden and Thomas to keep him company,
For that's the place where traitor's ought to be.

The most damaging accusations against MacDonald come from L. MacNeill Weir in his book *The Tragedy of Ramsay MacDonald* (1, i). In this he suggests that MacDonald was never a Socialist, but a Liberal, an opportunist, that he schemed to ditch the Labour Government and that he betrayed his supporters. The whole book is supported by about six hundred pages of cartoons and conjectural statements. There is little precise evidence of an incriminating nature offered. Yet this book has provided the basis of how the Labour Party has viewed MacDonald since the 1930s. David Marquand's reinterpretation of MacDonald in 1977 (1, ii) is far more sober and balanced in approach suggesting that MacDonald was as good a Socialist as any other Labour leader of the time, that he was a principled opportunist, and that no evidence exists that he schemed to abandon the Labour Government, though he may have betrayed those who trusted in him.

Despite Marquand's detailed reassessment of MacDonald, the impression still survives that MacDonald was personally responsible for all the events of 1931. Nevertheless, the body of available evidence tends to suggest that Marquand's view is the more accurate.

Operating in a climate where unemployment had risen from just over one million to about three million between 1929 and 1931, owing to the world recession following the 1929 Wall Street Crash, the second Labour Government was faced with the rapidly rising cost of providing unemployment benefits. It set up the Gregory Commission, a Royal Commission, in December 1930, to examine the whole issue of unemployment and the financing of the Unemployment Insurance Fund. When it reported in June 1931 it called for reductions of up to 30 per cent in benefits. In addition, to avoid censure, the Labour Government accepted the formation of an all-party committee under Sir George May, to advise Snowden how to balance the budget. When it reported at the end of July 1931, it suggested that there would be a budget deficit of £120 millions and advocated the £67 millions of savings should come from increases in unemployment insurance contributions, changes in benefits, and a reduction of the standard benefit by 20 per cent.

The MacDonald diaries (2), admittedly a partial source, reflect upon the above financial difficulties and the way in which Snowden placed pressure on MacDonald and the Cabinet to win support for his advocacy of balanced budgets and the continuance of free trade. There are suggestions that MacDonald would have contemplated protection and taking Britain off the Gold Standard had it not been for the fact that such action would have forced the resignation of the Chancellor of the Exchequer and precipitated further financial chaos. What emerges from MacDonald's diaries is the intense debate within Cabinet which resulted in the split over the introduction of a 10 per cent cut in unemployment benefits on 23 August 1931. MacDonald's diaries do not suggest that he schemed to bring about the end of the Labour Government, nor do they suggest that he had much control over the exact timing of events.

The Cabinet Conclusions (3) tend to confirm this impression. The main thrust of these records of Cabinet meetings is that Snowden was demanding that the budget should be balanced, that the Cabinet Economy Committee agreed to a package of £78 million in cuts but that, despite the pressure from the Opposition leaders and the international bankers, the full Cabinet would not agree to cuts of more than £56 million. On 23 August 1931, the Cabinet finally divided over the suggestion that a 10 per cent cut should be made in unemployment benefits.

When the National Government was formed, MacDonald took with him a few of his former Labour ministers. Philip Snowden was one of these and continued as Chancellor of the Exchequer until the general election of October 1931, accepting the need to resolve the economic crisis (4). It was Snowden who eventually signed the document, on 22 September 1931, to take Britain off the Gold Standard, an action which paved the way for protectionism. He remained a member of the National Government until the autumn of 1932 when he resigned over the protectionist measures implied by the Ottawa Conference. From then onwards he was one of MacDonald's sternest critics and, having been raised to the House of Lords in November 1931, proceeded to use the Lords to launch his personal attacks upon MacDonald (5).

The available evidence suggests that MacDonald did not plan to replace the second Labour Government with a National Government. Nevertheless, the myth lingers on, perpetuated by the memory of what came after – Labour's electoral disaster in the general election of October 1931. In the final analysis, MacDonald had not remained true to the party and the movement which had supported him. It is for this reason that the Labour Party have assigned him to a 'traitor's grave'. Nevertheless, one must always remember the reflection of C.L. Mowat ('Ramsay MacDonald and the Labour Par ', in A. Briggs and J.

Saville (eds), *Essays in Labour History*), that 'If the Labour Party condemns MacDonald it condemns itself for having chosen and retained him as leader'.

1) *MacDonald and the collapse of the second Labour Government, 1931*
(i)   *L. MacNeill Weir's personal attack upon Ramsay MacDonald*
(L. MacNeill Weir, *The Tragedy of Ramsay MacDonald*)

(p. xi) MacDonald was always the most accommodating of Socialists. His Socialism was of the kind that Sir William Harcourt meant when he said on a famous occasion: 'We are all Socialists now.' His Socialism is that far-off Never-Never-Land, born of vague aspiration and described by him in picturesque generalities. It is a Turner landscape of beautiful colours and glorious indefiniteness. He saw it, not with a telescope, but with a kaleidoscope. It is as real and remote as the garden of Hesperides. Anyone can believe in it without sacrifice or even inconvenience.

It is evident now that MacDonald never really accepted the Socialist faith of a classless society, based on unselfish service. It can be seen now that he could never have at heart believed in the principles of Brotherhood and self-denial, which are the bases of Socialism.

'Just for handful of silver he left us,
Just for a ribbon to stick in his coat.'

(p. xii) It is MacDonald's conduct after he had climbed clear of the swamp, after he had reached a position of safety, his primary needs satisfied, that calls for the strongest condemnation. Then he had no excuse, and then it was that he turned on those who had befriended him, and sought to drive deeper into the slough of poverty the people who had helped him out.

(p. 322) It was generally believed that the setting up of the 'National' Government was an affair of extreme suddennness and urgency. It was understood to be a hasty improvisation but in the month of June the Lobby journalists knew definitely that arrangements had already been made to set up a 'National' Government; the time was known, too, and was given as early autumn; even the names of those who were to be in it were bruited about. It was known that Thomas was to be in the Cabinet of the 'National' Government.

(p. 327) Although the project to set up a 'National' Government had been planned long ahead, it had, of course, to be kept secret. If it had been known, the whole scheme would be wrecked. The essence of the plan was that the 'National' Government was an improvisation which had to be set up hastily and quite unexpectedly to meet a sudden grave emergency.

(p. 383) [Following the split of the Labour Cabinet over the issue of reducing unemployment benefit by 10 per cent, MacDonald asked for the resignations of the Labour Cabinet.] The members of the Labour Cabinet naturally assumed on that Sunday night, 23 August, that Mr. Baldwin would be asked to form a government. But it is significant that MacDonald had something quite different in view. Without a word of consultation with his Cabinet colleagues, without even informing them of his intention to set up a National Government with himself as Prime Minister, he proceeded to carry out his long-thought-out plan.

(ii) *David Marquand's more balanced and less critical assessment of the events of 1931 and MacDonald's role in the collapse of the second Labour Government in August 1931 and the formation of the National Government*

(D. Marquand, *Ramsay MacDonald*)

(p. 791) The two charges most often brought against him are that he was a vain and snobbish social climber, who betrayed his party and ideals, and that he was an impractical dreamer, who could not cope with the problems of government. The truth is more complicated [. . .] His political creed was undoubtedly utopian, and his platform rhetoric, like that of most of the great orators of his generation, strikes a modern ear as sentimental. But . . . he was quite capable of mastering formidable masses of detail, and his approach to economic problems was surprisingly hard-headed. [. . .] The same is true of his actions in August, 1931. The attitudes and beliefs which guided him during the disputes that broke the Labour Government were the attitudes and beliefs which had guided him for most of his political life. Once he had come to the conclusion that it would be a disaster for the country if the parity were abandoned, he had no choice but to act as he did. If he had acted differently, he would have been untrue to his convictions and untrue to himself.

(p. 641) Yet later Labour suggestions that he was glad to break with the party and no longer cared what it thought of him do not fit the facts. [. . .] The only clear conclusions that emerge from his behaviour immediately after the Buckingham Palace conference are that he had no plan for the future, and that he was in no condition to make one. All his energies had gone into deciding whether or not to form a National Government; he had given little thought to the problems he would face if he decided in favour.

2) *Extracts from the MacDonald Diaries relating to the economic crisis of 1931 and the events of August 1931*
(PRO, 30/69, 1753, MacDonald Diaries, 1910–1937)

8 March 1931 ... illness of Chancellor important, not only because he should be getting on with this Budget but because he ought to be at Cabinet for decisions on quota & Ottawa policy. His absence puts me in a fix because alternatives are: 1. Delay further. 2. Decide against him in his absence. Whenever the Cabinet has been united & someone was free to pursue a policy we have been a great success; but Cabinet hopelessly divided on home economic policy & we have been paralysed. Conf. with Sec. to Treasury on work of Budget.

27 April 1931 Budget. Chancellor showed no sign of having been ill except that he was quicker in his movement of body & somewhat flatter in his speech. Difficult to say whether the quietness of the House owing to approval & relief or restraint & sympathy. My first impression is that his Budget is too much of a stop gap, of a waiting in expectation of economy & propriety. A Tory said: "We are thankful it is not much worse"; a Left-wing Labour "If that is the Government policy, the sooner it goes out the better."

31 July 1931 House rose with a feeling that it was not for long. As international broker we are in a precarious position.

7 August Met Chancellor on Tuesday 11.20 am ... found gloomier prospects than ever. Bank considering how much more

it is justified using or whether it is hopeless to try to keep £; situation got beyond them & only Govt. can act. We pressed them to say what they meant. Reply: the failure to balance Budget is forfeiting confidence in sterling; something should be done at once to prove the Budget is to be balanced. A renewed declaration not enough but at same time full details not required. H. of C. might meet. I pointed out how damaging that might be. [. . .] They said something would have to be done within a few days – a fortnight at the outside. They wanted to see representatives of the opposition & we said they ought. [. . .] They discussed with Chancellor & decided to call Cab. Sub. Cmm. for tomorrow afternoon.

13 August 1931   Yesterday hopeful day in the City owing to work done here. May be strengthened by Sub. Comm. Yesterday I proposed "the 1924 standards" as a basis for working out schemes of economy & value for money eg cuts in unempt. pay and reductions in fixed income by taxation.

17 August 1931   Chancellor has found week-end all too brief & I found a letter from him saying he would not be able to meet Liberals & Tories tomorrow as arranged & I sent a letter to Chamberlain, Samuel [. . .]
At last 4 o'clock & the meeting of the Cabinet Sub Committee on Economy,. . . When we began Henderson at once showed his hand. He wanted the whole scheme. I pointed out that we had met to make it. He objected to the sacrifice being on one side – his reason alleged being that first or last we should have to discuss them. Then he launched out at eloquence on the inadequacy of the unemployed grants & what we had all said for 30 yrs. We pointed out that this was a special crisis & we hoped temporary; that if the income was not there there could not be the expenditure. He could not reply but lapsed into sulking silence for a time & we went on with business. It was a bitter day . . . We dispersed at 10 o'clock having ticked down expenditure provisionally by £87,000,000 per annum.

18 August 1931   Long discussion 10.30 – 1 & 2.30 – 6, reducing our salaries & imposing new taxes. I am disappointed with the scheme & disheartened. Discussed a reventue tax, 4 in favour & the Chancellor against.

20 August 1931 [. . .] New taxation (direct) too heavy to Lib & Tories. Shocked by deficit of £170 m. Said little of deficit but evidently would not look at direct taxation.

21 August 1931 One more crammed day. 9.30 Chancellor, 10 Opposition leaders (Hoare for Baldwin) 11 Committee 3 TUC & Lab. Pty Executive 4.30 Neville Chamberlain 5.30 Sir H. Samuel, & Graham to dine . . .

At the TUC meeting the usual pompous & self-important (of the type produced by an inferiority complex) attitude was observed & practically after hearing myself & Snowden they broke up the meeting & retired to deliberate their attitude. 8.15 pm telephone message came from them saying they had deliberated, their conclusions were not in writing but that deputation appointed to put them before Cabinet Committee. We asked them to come at 9.30. They included . . . Citrine, Bevin, Pugh, Walkden MP. Their statement was that they were not to support the policy introduced by us in the afternoon, that we could balance the Budget by taxing the rentier, suspending Sinking Fund(all) & such like, but no economies. Chancellor replied & I observed that all I had to say was that their observations did not touch our problem arising out of immediate financial necessity. They withdrew. It was practically a declaration of war.

I was very tired & snatched a few minutes rest whilst Henderson once more told us what he had proposed days ago & how everything had been initiated by him – except the things opposed by his TUC people. He surrendered. He proposed to balance the Budget with insignificant economies, keeping the unemployed assistance what it is now . . . suspending Sinking Fund (which he stated many times was his proposal made days ago admitting that he was only now aware that some were statutory) & putting on a revenue tariff. How tired of it all one feels. We had a rather pointless discussion without concentration on the point of any importance: "Are we to go on?" [. . .]

22 August 1931 [. . .] If we yield to the TUC we shall never be able to call our bodies, or souls or intelligence our own. 10 Cabinet. Reported the TUC position. [. . .] Complex disagreement on unemployment [. . .] Mr. Tariff Revenue was in the background all the time. . . . I tended opinion on 'no change' in

unemployt pay, 5 % reduction or 10 % reduction. Finally as between 10 % reduction & no change the Cabinet was divided. [Also met the Opposition leaders on the same day.]

23 August 1931 (Sunday) Yesterday 9.30. Cabinet met & after a long discussion decided to allow Snowden & myself to put a proposal of 10% cut in unemployment benefits with promise of further attempts to find Budget Savings in grant to Local Authorities. . . to bankers & the Opposition leaders. [MacDonald went to see the King] King most friendly & expressed thanks & confidence. I then reported the situation. [. . .] He said that he thought I was only person who could carry the country through. I said that I did not share his belief. [. . .] I said that there would be no election till the crisis was well over & then that so far as I could see, & on the assumption of resignation, no man could avoid it then. . . 11.30 saw Hopwood & Harvey & they reported progress – Henderson, 2 others . . . met after Cabinet yesterday & decided to resign on 10% cut. [. . .] I commit political suicide & save the crisis. If there is no other way I shall do it as cheerfully as an ancient Jap. [. . .] Henderson backed up now by six others refuses to have any acts. TUC too strong. Cabinet resigns.

24 August 1931 P.M. to take resignation to King. The result due to Henderson changing his mind. At Llandrudod he and I agreed to equality of sacrifice, & cut in the dole and a revenue tariff. The T.U.C. didn't agree so Henderson gave way partly influenced no doubt by his quarrel with the Prime Minister and his desire for leadership, but he wasn't strong enough for the crisis. The culminating day. 10 King. Decided only Nat. Govt. will do to meet the crisis. [. . .] It was plain that I should be left almost alone with Snowden, Thomas, Sankey.

11 September 1931 Snowden's new Budget yesterday. Great triumph.

18 September 1931 Saw Samuel & Baldwin & discussed election further. Explained my position. 1. Election may be good political tactics but wd produce financial crisis. 2. What issue? Split on tariffs. 3. What result? National majority would be a Tory one. I am willing to help reduce Opposition numbers – but am not Tory & will not be.

21 September 1931   Officially off gold standard.

25 November 1931   Saw H. of Lords the In. of Snowden. . . . has introduced a fine dignified figure. S. an imp, his embodiment of the sardonic.

3) *The financial crisis of 1931 as recorded in the Cabinet Conclusions* (Cab. 23, PRO)

Cabinet Meeting,   30 July 1931, 4.0 pm.

Agenda – May Report

10th Item Cabinet – Report of Committee on National Expenditure appointed 17 March 1931 under Sir George May

Agreed Cabinet Committee composed of P.M., Chancellor of the Exchequer, Secretary of State for Foreign Affairs, Secretary of State for Dominion Affairs and President of the Board of Trades should meet to consider the Report.

Cabinet Meeting,   19 August 1931, 11. am.

11. am – 10.30 pm [. . .]

PM, C. of E. explained the gravity of the situation.

In the course of the discussion it became clear that while the Cabinet were prepared, though well reluctant, to accept on a temporary measure to meet the present emergency, certain of the economies set out in C P 203 (31) (subject in certain cases to further consulation between the C. of E. & Department Ministers concerned), the Cabinet were not prepared to entertain the main recommendations of the May Committee, in regard to Unemployment Insurance, including the proposal (reported by the Cabinet Cttee) for a reduction of benefits, and also a suggestion that persons who have fallen out of insurance should be handed over to the Public Assistance Authorities. It was also argued amongst other things that in the case of Transitional Benefit, the arrangements in contemplation would involve financial burden on the local authorities which the great majority of these authorities would be unable to bear.

Conclusion

(1)   The Cabinet adopted the Conclusion reached by the Cabinet Cttee that the Budget must be balanced by the application of the principle of a common sacrifice and effort.

Approval of indirect taxation in light of the explanation of Chancellor of the Exchequer.

Certain members of the Cabinet instructed that their acceptance of the proposed economies was conditioned on effect being given in principle to the proposals concerning direct taxation.
[. . .]

Cabinet Meeting, 20 August 1931 8.30 pm

[. . .] All Opposition leaders had made it clear that they could not possibly contemplate the imposition of new taxation of the order of £100 million. [. . .]

Chancellor of the Exchequer . . . The situation today was that Unemployment Insurance economies were put at £22 million & other economies at £30 million – or £52 million in all – leaving a gap to be filled by taxation of £118 million. [. . .] In this connection the Cabinet were reminded that the value of Unemployment benefit to-day was over 30 per cent higher than the 1924 value, and that the value had been accepted as adequate by the then Labour Government at a time when the Budgets were showing handsome surpluses.

Cabinet Meeting, 21 August 1931, 10.0 am.

[Chancellor of Exchequer's account of meeting between Cab. Committee on the Report of the Committee on National Expenditure & a Committee of General Council of TUC.] The meeting had been a friendly one, and Mr. Citrine, who acted as spokeman for the Committee pointed out that in the view of the General Council, the Government had been mistaken in their method of approaching the problem. All through his statement, and in subsequent discussion, it appeared that the members of the General Council had no real appreciation of the seriousness of the situation, the statement appeared to be based upon a pre-crisis mentality, and the objections raised to the proposals were those which members of the Cabinet themselves would have taken had the circumstances been quite normal. With regard to the suggested economies, Mr. Citrine had stated that the General Council were opposed to any interference with the existing terms and conditions of the Unemployment Insurance Scheme, including the limitation of benefit to 26 weeks . . . The Chancellor of the Exchequer added that he had replied to the point raised at some length, but that it must be realised that the Trades Union General Council were not prepared to accept the scheme of economies which had been proposed by the Government.

Cabinet Meeting, 22 August 1931, 9.30 am. .... [MacDonald on representatives of the Bank of England who] made it quite clear that, if economies suggested represented the Government's final word, the scheme would be of no value. They pointed out that an analysis of the figures showed that against the total deficit, real savings in expenditure only amounted £42 million. The other so-called economies were merely additional burdens which, while they would ease the Exchequer position, really involved further taxation of the employer and the workman. It could not be too clearly recognised that foreign lenders regarded the heavy financial burden on industry of the Unemployment Insurance Scheme as impairing the security of their loans. In the considered opinion of the bankers the loans would not only not produce the required effect, but would probably worsen the position by further diminishing confidence, [. . .] All the Party leaders looked for economies which would in the aggregate be substantially greater than the figure of £56 million proposed. They urged, however, that the real weakness of the proposals was the failure to secure adequate economies on Unemployment Insurance. [. . .]

In reply to the question relative to the Sinking Fund proposal, the CHANCELLOR OF THE EXCHEQUER informed the Cabinet that the Leaders of the Conservative Party, and also the Representatives of the Bankers, had stated that any attempt of this kind to camouflage the true position would be at once detected, and that it was of paramount importance that the Budget should be balanced in an honest fashion, and not by recourse to borrowing. [. . .] In his, the Chancellor of the Exchequer's, view the first question for decision was whether the Cabinet would now review their findings of the previous day and add a further £25–30 million of economies to the present figure of £56 million gross. [. . .]

There could be no possible question that, of the reasons for the present crisis, much the most serious was the huge and rapidly growing expenditure on Unemployment Insurance which must inevitably be dealt with by either the present or some future Government.

Cabinet Meeting, 22 August, 2.30 pm. [MacDonald, the Prime Minister reported to the Cabinet on a meeting with the Opposition leaders where the suggestion of further economies, including a 10 per cent cut in Unemployment Insurance Benefit was put to them. After his report, he and the Chancellor of the Exchequer were instructed to contact the Bank of England about the proposals, which in turn would contact the US Federal Reserve Bank authorities.]

The Party leaders were unable to give a definite reply beyond indicating that the question was one which, in their opinion, should be put to the financial authorities responsible for raising the contemplated loan in New York and Paris.

Cabinet Meeting, 23 August 1931, 7.0 pm. [MacDonald reported that Sir E. Harvey had reported to him that Mr. Harrison, of Federal Reserve Bank had agreed that the additional economies, including the 10 per cent reduction in Unemployment Benefit, would be sufficient to satisfy those raising the proposed loan in New York. The issue then became whether or not the Cabinet was prepared to agree to the additional economies. Each member of the Cabinet expressed his views and it was clear, though no vote was recorded, that the Cabinet was split and that there would be resignations. There was partial acceptance of the proposals but] adoption of the part [10 per cent cut in unemployment benefits] as part and parcel of the scheme would involve the resignation of certain Ministers of the Government. [It was therefore announced that MacDonald would meet the King and Baldwin and Sir H. Samuel the following morning.]

Cabinet Meeting, 24 August 1931, 12 noon. [The formal resignation of the Government was announced.] The proposal was that His Majesty would invite certain individuals as individuals to take upon their shoulders the burden of carrying on the Government, and Mr. Baldwin and Sir Herbert Samuel had stated that they were now prepared to act accordingly. [. . .]

It had been agreed that at the General Election which would follow the end of the emergency period, there would be no "coupons" pools or other Party arrangements. [. . .]

The Prime Minister added that he had obtained assurances to the effect that the general scheme of economies to be placed before Parliament by the new administration would be on the lines of the proposals which had been submitted to the Bankers, including the ten per cent cut in Unemployment Insurance. In effect, therefore, there would be no serious departure from the scheme which at their meeting on August 22nd (Cabinet 45 (31)) the Cabinet had authorised the Chancellor and himself to submit tentatively to the Leaders of the Opposition Parties and to the bankers.

Cabinet Meeting, 3 September 1931, 3.0 pm. [. . .] Mr. Snowden emphasised the importance of preparing the public mind in a general way for a considerable increase in taxation. It should be emphasised that such increase was unavoidable but would be accompanied by very large economies.

Cabinet Meeting, 17 September 1931, 8.30 pm. [The financial situation remained unsettled.] The bankers had reported a deterioration in the financial situation due to an increase in the withdrawal from London during the last few days.

Cabinet Meeting, 21 September 1931, 11.30 am. On 19 September the Bank of England made a formal application to be relieved of their obligation to sell gold under the provisions of the Gold Standard Act, 1925.

Cabinet Meeting, 22 September 1931, 11. 0 am. Order made by the Treasury under Section I (3) of the Gold Standard (Amendment) Act, 1931.

Signed by Philip Snowden
George Penny

4) *Philip Snowden on the formation of the National Government*
(P. Snowden, *An Autobiography*, p.955)

When the members of the Labour Cabinet were leaving after the Prime Minister announced that we had agreed to form a National Government, he asked me and Mr. Thomas and Lord Sankey to remain behind. We then had a frank conversation about the new situation which had so unexpectedly arisen. He asked us if we were prepared to join him in the Government which was to be formed. In view of my position as Chancellor of the Exchequer, and the exceptional responsibility I had for helping to get the country out of its difficulties, I felt that there was no other course open to me than to assist the new Government provided I could get certain assurances as to its character and its purpose. The definite assurances which were given to me were:

(1) That the new Administration would not exist for a longer period than to dispose of the emergency, and that when that was achieved the political parties would assume their respective positions.

(2) That the Administration would not be a Coalition Government in the general sense of the term, but a National Government for one purpose only.

(3) That as soon as the financial crisis had been settled there should be a General Election, and at that Election there would be no merging of political parties and no 'Coupon' or other party arrangements.

(4) That the Administration which was being formed would not propose any party legislation of a controversial character, but would confine itself to the one purpose for which it was being formed.

I had not the least intention then of the developments which followed later. It never entered my mind that this meant the permanent separation from my former colleagues in the Labour Party. I expected that, though we had differed on what, after all, was a comparatively trivial matter, we should be able to resume our former cooperation in the Labour Party when the emergency legislation had been passed.

5) *Philip Snowden's personal attacks upon MacDonald following his resignation in the autumn of 1932*

(i) (*Yorkshire Post*, 25 May 1933, reporting Snowden's speech in the House of Lords, 24 May 1933)

Whether the reason for that [the National Government's failure to offer a clear economic policy] is that the Government have no policy or whether it is due to the constitutional inability of the Prime Minister to make a clear statement I do not know ... I have referred to that speech [a recent speech by MacDonald] and there is not from beginning to end a word about the

Government's policy at the World Economic Conference. [...]

I would suggest to the Cabinet that they should look into the case of the Prime Minister, not only in his own interests, but in the interests of the country for it is a positive danger to the country that its affairs should be in the hands of a man who, every time he speaks, exposes his ignorance and incapacity.

(ii) (*The Times*, 4 July 1934, reporting Snowden's speech in the House of Lords, 3 July 1934)

At the last General Election millions of Labour, Liberal and free trade votes were given to the National Government candidates – because the electors believed Mr. Baldwin's statement that free trade and protection were not the issue at the election. Now the Government were boasting that they had killed free trade and established tariffs for a generation to come. [...] 'He had been betrayed.' That mattered little, but the country had been betrayed, and millions of electors who trusted to the statements of the party leaders had lost their confidence in the faith and honesty of their political leaders. [...]

When the House of Commons were discussing this question [the suspension of the taxation of Land Values] there were demands that the Prime Minister should be present, but he was spending his time in Downing Street listening to a concert. The Prime Minister had broken his silence once in regard to the subject in a letter which he had written to the Committee for the Taxation of Land Values. That letter was described by a Liberal member of the House of Commons as a piece of nauseating hypocracy. He [Lord Snowden] thought that was an apt description and he could not improve upon it. [...]

The Truth is that the Tories have got the power, and they mean to use it. At the next election the slogan will be National Government or Socialist Government. At that election the Tories will have no use for the Prime Minister except as an exhibition on Tory platforms ... as a one-time Socialist who has seen the error of his ways, and has found salvation and his spiritual home in the Tory Party. He will be used for the same purpose as the reformed drunkard is used at the temperance meeting (Laughter). The Prime Minister told us at a recent meeting that he stood by everything he had said as a Socialist. Let him act upon that, and then he will see what use his Tory colleagues will have for him. He told us in the same speech that what the country needs is honest political leadership. I quite agree.

LABOUR'S FALL AND RISE, 1931–1945

MacDonald's defection and the disastrous October 1931 General Election were a trauma for the Labour Party. The confidence gained in the 1920s was suddenly swept away. Yet, within fourteen years, in July 1945, the Labour Party came to power with 393 MPs, giving it a substantial majority in Parliament for the first time in its history. This dramatic revival had occurred owing to a combination of factors – the most obvious being the resilience of political support for Labour, its improved organisation and the rising collectivist spirit of the Second World War.

The 1931 General Election had reduced Labour to 52 MPs, only 10 more than it had achieved at the December 1910 General Election. Nevertheless, the Party quickly recovered from its defeat. Its parliamentary representation rose from 52 seats to 154 between 1931 and 1935, and the Labour vote in 1935, at 8,328,491, was only about 64,000 less than it had been in 1929. Indeed, Labour's national percentage of the poll rose from 37.1 per cent in 1929 to 37.9 per cent in 1935. There had been some losses for Labour at the 1931 municipal elections, but these had been largely recovered in 1932 (1, i). The Labour Party was clearly taking up the challenges posed by the National Government (1, ii). It began 'A Million New Members and Power Campaign' and within a year its individual membership had risen by over 100,000 (1, iv). In January 1933 it set up a central By-Election Insurance Fund to help the needy constituencies to put forward candidates and 'Victory for Socialism' conferences were held throughout the country (1, iii).

During this process of recovery it is clear that the Labour Party was faced with the serious problem of the challenge of fascism in Britain and Europe. As far as British fascism was concerned its policy was to ignore it, rather than to face it with violent conflict on the streets as the Communist Party had decided to do. Given the basic unimportance of Oswald Mosley and the British Union of Fascists it is hardly surprising that William Leach and Fred Jowett should play down the wisdom of those who wished to fight fascism on the streets (2, i, ii). The Labour Party 1934 circular, which revealed the essential thinness of fascist support even in its strongholds, tended to confirm the correctness of the Labour Party's position (3). It was only in areas where there was a substantial Jewish presence that the local Labour parties were forced into taking more determined action (7).

The Labour Party was quite right to play down the fascist challenge in Britain. What they could not do is ignore the threat of European fascism.

Throughout the inter-war years Labour politicians had been concerned with the preservation of peace. They posed numerous questions. Could European peace be guaranteed by disarmament? How could Germany be prevented from entering another major international conflict? Could French fears of, and hostility towards, Germany be removed? To these and similar questions they offered three policies for peace in Europe: disarmament, collective security operating through the League of Nations, and the restoration to Germany of her territories stripped away by the Treaty of Versaille. It is widely believed that these policies would provide the basis of peaceful co-existence between nations. Yet mutual distrust between France and Germany persisted, Hitler rose to power, the Spanish Civil War occurred and the Italians intervened in Abyssinia. Some Labour politicians continued to cling to their previous peace strategies but by 1935 the majority had come to accept the need to challenge European fascism (4).

At the 1935 Labour Party Conference, Ernest Bevin swept away the protests of George Lansbury and got the conference to support the demand for collective security through the League of Nations' sanctions, including, if necessary, military sanctions against Italian aggression in Abyssinia.

The Spanish Civil War, occasioned by Franco's invasion of Spain with his fascist forces in July 1936, threw the Labour Party into even more confusion. At first, the Party supported the Non-Intervention policy being advocated by the National Government. But at the Party conference in October 1936 there was condemnation for this policy since it was being flouted by many of the major powers – though even this condemnation did not go far enough for some of those present (5, i). In the end, however, the Labour Party was not prepared to go beyond advocating the raising of relief help for the Spanish Republic (5, ii), a policy which was generally supported by the trade unions (5, iii).

There were some within the Labour Party who were insistent that the only way to deal with European fascism was to join forces with other socialist and communist societies in a 'United Front' against fascism, or even in a 'popular front' between all the political parties who were prepared to oppose fascism. The 'United Front' policy was strongly supported by the Communist Party. However, only the Socialist League and Stafford Cripps, within the Labour Party, were prepared to advocate such a policy. The Socialist League was a small party, or group, which had been formed from those ILP members who had decided to stay in the Labour Party in 1932. Eventually, the Party took action against the Socialist League and its supporters (6, i, ii) and it was forced to disband in May 1937.

The Labour Party firmly supported the British government's declaration of war on Germany on 3 September 1939, agreed to an 'Electoral Truce', but refused to join the Chamberlain government in the prosecution of the war. It did not enter the Coalition Government until May 1940, when Winston Churchill had replaced Chamberlain as Prime Minister. The Party appears to have done well out of the growth of wartime collectivism and was very strongly in favour of measures which were soon to become known as 'War Socialism'. It strongly favoured the implementation of something along the lines of the Beveridge Report of 1942, *Social Insurance and Allied Services*.

Nominally, this report was the product of the Social Insurance Committee set up by the Ministry of Health in May 1941, but in fact it was almost entirely the work of William Beveridge. In it, he gave systematic shape to ideas about social security. Social insurance was to be reorganised to provide a national minimum income and his proposals depended upon three assumptions: a national health service, family allowances, and full employment guaranteed by government. It was a controversial and comprehensive scheme which threatened to reorganize the whole structure of society.

Churchill was rather suspicious about where such demands might lead but the Labour Party was more supportive and Attlee sent a memorandum to Churchill insisting upon the need to accept something like the Beveridge Report, whatever its deficiencies might be (8, i). The Labour Party strongly supported the general intentions behind the Beveridge Report, although it soon became clear that some Labour politicians were concerned at the limited nature of some of its proposals, particularly the notion that it would take twenty years to build up to a position whereby the full old age pension rate would be paid (8, ii).

By 1945 the Labour Party was demonstrably the party most likely to introduce the social reforms which were essential if Britain was to avoid the mistakes of the inter-war years. In addition, it had revealed its ability to operate in government. The electorate concurred and the Labour Party won the general election of July 1945, called within two months of the end of the European war, by a substantial majority: 393 seats to the Conservatives 213. The Liberals had won only 12 seats. It had fought and won the election on its programme *Let Us Face the Future*, which stressed the need to avoid the failures of the 1930s and to introduce domestic legislation which would include the nationalisation of industries, full employment and improved social services (9). Nevertheless, it should be remembered that its victory was the culmination of years of sedulous hard work which had gone on since the 1930s. But it presented the Party with a serious challenge for it now had to demonstrate that it was capable of implementing its socialist programme – one to meet the social optimism which had helped sweep it to power in 1945.

1) *Labour's Revival after 1931*
(i) *Relative Success of Labour Candidates in Municipal Elections: 1931–2*
(J. Stevenson and C. Cook, *The Slump*, p.114)

1931	Candidates	Elected	1932	Candidates	Elected
Con.	465	350	Con.	490	218
Lib.	154	107	Lib.	174	87
Lab.	709	149	Lab.	836	836
Ind.	308	154	Ind.	329	106

(ii)   *Labour's Challenge*
(*Bradford Pioneer*, 26 August 1932)

The Labour Party is now challenging capitalism along a wide front, and this fight is only just beginning. The desertion of leaders, the disappointment of office, the skilful manipulation of finance by Labour's enemies, the misunderstanding of electors, the appeal of capitalist politicians to a spurious patriotism, all these have taught the movement a much needed lesson. Political strategy of a high order must follow on the heels of disillusionment. [. . .]

A Labour Government will obtain a Socialist mandate only if the electors are made much more familiar with the details of such proposals as those the Labour Party is to discuss at its Annual Conference this year.

(iii)   *Victory for Socialism Conference, 1934*
(*Bradford Pioneer*, 29 June 1934)

Victory at the next election means getting voters now. Mr. Foster Sunderland . . . saw the Labour Party policy as the only solution of the world's problems to-day. [. . .] George Dallas, ex MP, told the meeting that the Labour Party must have a mandate for power. 'They are determined to speed up the Parliamentary machine. . . . The unemployed have no hope under capitalism.'

(iv)   *Growth of Membership*
(J. Stevenson and C. Cook, *The Slump*, pp.115–16)

By the late autumn of 1932, the party's organisation and morale had begun to make a noticeable recovery. Labour's new 'A Million New Members and Power' campaign had made much headway, both in terms of publicity and in concrete terms with new members. By the end of the year Shepherd, the National Agent, was able to inform the N.E.C. that memberhip had increased by 100,000 with especially good increases in London, the North and the Midlands.

2) *Labour Party and Independent Labour Party hostility towards the use of violence in dealing with Fascism*
(i)   *William Leach criticising those who ignored the Labour Party line*
(*Bradford Pioneer*, 4 January 1935)

I notice my friend the President of the Bradford Trades Council

113

has been expressing disappointment that he was prevented by the police from leading an army of counter-demonstrators to Sir Oswald's Bradford Meeting late 1934 even though Sir Oswald's bodyguard had been equipped with steel waistcoat and knuckle-duster and other equipment.

I cannot for the life of me see how these can be effective ways to combat the growth of Fascist opinion. I think it would have precisely the contrary effect.

(ii) *Fred Jowett of the ILP expressing his opposition to using violence* (A.F. Brockway, *Socialism over Sixty Years: The Life of Jowett of Bradford*, p.310)

Two things I regard as being certain to help the growth of Fascism in this country. One is for anti-Fascists to compete with it otherwise than by methods of reason. Attempts to suppress Fascism by organised disorder or riotous assembly will only afford excuse for more violence and for police intervention, which under present direction will be mainly for Protection for Fascism.

The other is discredit of democratic institutions. What a disastrous thing it is for opponents of Fascism to help Fascism by bringing these institutions into discredit, through failure to use them or by deriding them, may be judged by the need of them in Germany now.

German Socialists, Left, Right, and Centre – a real united front – would joyfully welcome back their democratic institutions, and would use them if they had them.

3) *Responses to the Labour Party Circular on Fascism, 1934*
(Labour Party, LP / FAS / 34/20.1, 24.(1), 236)
City of Leeds Labour Party
It is said that one or two young Tory Councillors are sympathetic but I have no evidence that this is true.
Several prominent business men are associated and it is said that undue influence is being used to compel their employees to join. The Fascists have very large premises at Devonshire Hall. I am informed by one of our Councillors that they are surrounded with Barbed wire. He also says that about 50 or 60 fascists are drilling there regularly.

Another point of interest in Leeds is that the Fascists are threatening to oppose Vyvyan Adams, the Tory M.P. for West Leeds, who has been so active in the House of Commons in asking questions re the Fascists.

Harrogate

A kind of half-hearted support is offered by the younger elements of the Conservative Party. In Harrogate the local Fascist Organisation adopts different tactics to those applied in Industrial towns. At their meetings they invite criticism and appeal for questions, and appear to be gaining considerable ground in this area.

In expressing my own personal opinion I should be induced to say that the BUF is making considerable progress in and around Harrogate, and that their membership is being recruited very largely from the young people of the 'well to do class' of which there are a considerable number in Harrogate.

Huddersfield Divisional Labour Party

The True Meaning of Fascism

Blackshirt, Blackshirt, have you any plan?
Yes sir, yes sir, we've got two,
One's for the Master – the other's
for the Man.

The Brutality of the fascists

Last week there was a meeting of the fascists at Olympia, London. The vicious brutality shown then by the hired strong men of Mosley's private army, has made the name of fascism stink in the nostrils of all decent English people. This sort of thing is not to be tolerated here.

Fascist Development

This is nothing more or less than an attempt, by force, to keep things as they are, to prevent any changes in the industrial system of the country that are going to hurt the pockets of our big industrialists and capitalists. Where do you think all the money is coming from to keep the Mosley circus going? Not all of it from Mosley, no he is being subsidized by the capitalist class even as Mussolini, Hitler and Dollfuss were. And subsidized for one end, to prevent the mass of people from having their fair share in the wealth which they create. *That is fascism.* Nothing more or less. It cannot solve any of our problems, – unemployment, poverty, and all the accompanying miseries, – all it can do is to drive underground the opposition to these things, and to stifle the demands of the people for that fuller and finer life which they feel is their rightful due. [. . .]

MOSLEY'S MOVEMENT
MEANS
MENACE
and
MISERY
to the
MASSES

4) *The Labour Party Conference and Foreign Policy, 1935*
(Labour Party Conference, *Annual Report, 1935*)
[Ernest Bevin advocating economic sanctions against Italy over her invasion of Abyssinia, and opposing the opposition put up by Sir Stafford Cripps and George Lansbury, then leader of the Labour Party, was blunt in dealing with his opponents and winning his way.] I think the Movement ought to understand the Trade Union Congress's position. Let me remind the delegates that, when George Lansbury says what he has said today in the Conference, it is rather late to say it, and I hope this Conference will not be influenced by either sentiment or personal attachment. I hope you will carry no resolution of an emergency character telling a man with a conscience like Lansbury what he ought to do . . . It is placing the Executive and the Movement in an absolutely wrong position to be taking your conscience round from body to body asking to be told what you ought to do with it. . . I have had to sit in Conference with the Leader and come to decisions, and I am a democrat and I feel we have been betrayed.

5) *The Labour Party and the Spanish Civil War, 1936–1939*
(i) (C.P. Trevelyan, Labour Party Conference, *Annual Report, 1936*)
You are beggared of policy at this moment. [. . .] When the next great war now looming comes, and Japan and Germany crash in to try and destroy Soviet Russia, I hope the Labour Party will have some other policy to offer than sympathy accompanied by bandages and cigarettes.
(ii) (A statement circulated by the Labour Party and found in many Labour papers, such as the *Leeds Citizen*, 7 May 1937)
The dreadful sufferings of the Spanish people have reached a

climax of horror and shame in the criminal bombing of Guernica by German airplanes under the command of the rebel generals. [. . .] The General Council of the TUC and the National Executive Committee of the Labour Party condemned this action.

> 'The two National Committees pledge the organised working class movement to continue its humanitarian work in sending supplies of food and other necessities to the Spanish people, and renew their urgent appeal for further contributions to the International Solidarity Fund.'

(iii) (South Wales Miners' Federation poster appeal for the Spanish Republic 1938, reproduced in H. Francis and D. Smith, *The Fed*)

South Wales Miners' Federation
AID FOR THE SPANISH PEOPLE
AN APPEAL

The dreadful sufferings of the Spanish People, the ruthless slaughter of men, women and children, and the destruction of their homes by the rebel Franco and his FASCIST accomplices, ITALY and GERMANY, call for the active sympathy of ALL Workers.

The Fight of the SPANISH WORKERS against Fascism IS YOUR FIGHT.

The success of Fascism in Spain would endanger the liberties of the Workers in all Countries.

Fascism means the horrors of the Concentration Camps, Imprisonment and Death.

Help the Spanish People in their heroic struggle.

A Collection will be taken at your Colliery on FRIDAY NEXT, JULY 16th, to help to relieve distress caused by the Civil War.

THE SPANISH PEOPLE ARE GIVING THEIR LIVES, WE ASK YOU TO GIVE A GENEROUS CONTRIBUTION.

6) *'United Front'*

(i)   *Manifesto of the Socialist League, the Communist Party and the Independent Labour Party, February 1937*

(Published in many newspapers, such as the *Leeds Citizen*, 22 January 1937)

> Unity of all sections of the working-class movement.
>
> Unity in the struggle against Fascism, reaction and war, and against the National Government.
>
> Unity in the struggle for immediate demands and the return of Labour Government on the next stage in the advance of working-class power.
>
> Unity through the removal of all barriers between sections of the working-class movement, through the strengthening of trade unionism and co-operation, through the adoption of a fighting programme of mass struggle, through the democratisation of the Labour Party and the trade union movement.
>
> Unity through the framework of the Labour Party and the trade unions.

(ii)   *City of Leeds Labour Party*

(City of Leeds Labour Party, LP 4/1 – 4/16, Delegate Meeting of the General Committee, 19 May 1937, deposited in West Yorkshire Archives, Leeds Archives Department, Sheepscar, Leeds)

> The Secretary said that when Councillor Walker had taken the chair at the first public meeting held under the auspices of the 'Unity Campaign Committee' the National Executive Committee had not made public its intentions with regard to members of the Labour Party who associated themselves with the Campaign, no doubt in the hope that they would answer the appeal for loyalty and would cease to defy conference decisions. In the case of the meeting held 1st May, Councillor Walker was advertised as a speaker, and the National Executive Committee had now decided that it had no alternative but to take action against Labour Party members who spoke at such meetings. Consequently, the Secretary and the Chairman had addressed a letter to Councillor Walker drawing his attention to the facts. Councillor Walker had acknowledged receipt of the letter and as he had not spoken at the meeting, nothing further had been done on the matter.

7) *The Jewish reaction to the Anti-Semitism of the Fascists in Leeds*
(City of Leeds Labour Party, LP 4/1 – 4/16, Executive Committee meeting, 8 October 1936, deposited in West Yorkshire Archives, Leeds Archives Department, Sheepscar, Leeds)
Mr. Weinrib stated that his organisation was very concerned at the Anti-Semitic campaign of the fascists in Leeds, and urged the Labour Party to take steps to counteract it. Mr. Weinrib suggested open-air meetings, and the distribution of leaflets and lecturers at ward meetings on Palestine.
[. . .] It was resolved that a sub-committee consisting of the Chairman, Secretary, Councillor Beever, Councillor Peart and Mr. Hirst, should discuss with a sub-committee of the Jewish Socialist Labour Party the possibility of joint activity on the lines indicated.

8) *The Labour Party and the Beveridge Report, 1942*
(i)   *Attlee and the Beveridge Report*
(K. Harris, *Attlee*, pp. 220–1. This document would appear to be either in the University College Papers, Oxford or in the Churchill College Papers, Cambridge, which contain some of the Attlee correspondence with Churchill during the war)

> . . . I doubt whether in your inevitable and proper preoccupation with military problems you are fully cognisant of the extent to which decisions must be taken and implemented in the field of post war reconstruction *before* the end of the war. It is not that persons of particular views are seeking to make vast changes. These changes have already taken place. The changes from peacetime to wartime industry, the concentration of industry, the alterations in trade relations with foreign countries and with the Empire, to mention only a few factors, necessitate great readjustments and the new departures in the economic and industrial life of the nation. [. . .]
>
> I am certain that unless the Government is prepared to be as courageous in planning for the peace as it has been in carrying on the war, there is extreme danger of disaster when the war ends. I doubt if any of our colleagues who have been giving attention to the post war problems would be content with the mere preparation of paper schemes.
>
> I do not think the people of this country, especially the fighting

men would forgive us if we failed to take decisions to implement them because of some constitutional inhibition. I am not concerned at the moment with the Beveridge Report and its merits and demerits, but with the general principle ...

My contention is that if, as I think is generally agreed, it is not possible at the present time to have a general election. The Government and the present House of Commons must be prepared to take responsibility not only for winning the war but for taking the legislative and administrative action which is thought necessary for the post war situation.

(ii)   *Dalton and the Beveridge Report*
(H. Dalton, *The Second World War Diary of Hugh Dalton 1940–45*, ed. B. Pimlott, p.564)

... a fine stimulating document. ... I know Beveridge better than most people having served both under him and over him; that he is not 'one of us' and has no first hand knowledge of industrial conditions; that there are a number of things in his Report to which we could not subscribe, eg. the penalising of miners and railway workers because their jobs are inherently more risky than a carpenter's and the proposal to take twenty years to reach the appropriate rate of old age pensions.

9) *Let Us Face the Future, Labour electoral manifesto, 1945*
(Labour Party, *Let us Face the Future : A Declaration of Labour Policy for the Consideration of the Nation, 1945*)
[The industrial section of the manifesto dealt with public ownership of industry and services and with the planned management of the economy. The whole manifesto was dominated by the ideas of Herbert Morrison, who was later to be responsible for co-ordinating Labour's industrial and social programme through his office as Lord President of the Council between 1945 and 1950.]
What will the Labour Party do?

First, the whole of national resources, in land, material and labour must be fully employed. Production must be raised to the highest level and related to purchasing power. Over-production is not the cause of depression and unemployment; it is under-consumption that is responsible. It is doubtful whether we have ever, except in war, used the whole of our productive capacity. This must be corrected because, upon our ability to produce and organise a fair and generous distribution of the product, the standard of living of our people depends.

Secondly, a high and constant purchasing power can be maintained through good wages, social services and insurance and taxation which bears less heavily on the lower-income groups. But everybody knows that money and savings lose their value if prices rise, so rents and the prices of necessities of life will be controlled.

Thirdly, planned investment in essential industries and on houses, schools, hospitals and civic centres will occupy a large field of capital expenditure. A National Investment Board will determine social priorities and promote better timing in private investment. In suitable cases we would transfer the use of efficient Government factories from war production to meet the needs of peace. The location of new factories will be suitably controlled, and where necessary the Government will itself build factories. There must be no depressed areas in the New Britain.

Fourthly, the Bank of England with its financial powers must be brought under public ownership, and the operations of the other banks harmonised with industrial needs.

By these and other means full employment can be achieved. But a policy of Jobs for All must be associated with a policy of general economic expansion and efficiency as set out in the next section of this Declaration. Indeed, it is not enough to ensure that there are jobs for all. If the standard of life is to be high – as it should be – the standard of production must be high. This means that industry must be thoroughly efficient if the needs of the nation are to be met.

The Labour Party is a Socialist Party, and proud of it. Its ultimate purpose at home is the establishment of the Socialist Commonwealth of Great Britain – free, democratic, efficient, progressive, public-spirited, its material resources organised in the service of the British people.

But Socialism cannot come overnight, as the product of a week-end revolution. The members of the Labour Party, like the British people, are practical-minded men and women.

There are basic industries ripe and over-ripe for public ownership and management in the direct service of the nation. There are many smaller businesses rendering good service which can be left to go on with their useful work.

There are big industries not yet ripe for public ownership which must nevertheless be required by constructive supervision to further the nation's needs and not to prejudice national interests by restrictive anti-socialist monopoly or cartel agreements – caring for their own capital structures and profits at the cost of a lower standard of living for all.

In the light of these considerations, the Labour Party submits to the nation the following industrial programme:

1. Public ownership of the fuel and power industries. For a quarter of a century the coal industry, producing Britain's most precious national raw material, has been floundering chaotically under the ownership of many hundreds of independent companies. Amalgamation under public ownership will bring great economies in operation and make it possible to modernise production methods and to raise safety standards in every colliery in the country. Public ownership of gas and electricity undertakings will lower charges, prevent competitive waste, open the way for co-ordinated research and development, and lead to the reforming of uneconomic areas of distribution. Other industries will benefit.

2. Public ownership of inland transport. Co-ordination of transport services by rail, road, air and canal cannot be achieved without unification. And unification without public ownership means a steady struggle with sectional interests or the enthronement of a private monopoly, which would be a menace to the rest of industry.

3. Public ownership of iron and steel. Private monopoly has maintained high prices and kept inefficient high-cost plants in existence. Only if public ownership replaces private monopoly can the industry become efficient.

These socialised industries, taken over on a basis of fair compensation, to be conducted efficiently in the interests of consumers, coupled with proper status and conditions for the workers employed in them.

4. Public supervision of monopolies and cartels with the aim of advancing industrial efficiency in the service of the nation. Anti-social restrictive practices will be prohibited.

5. A firm and clear-cut programme for the export trade.

THE ATTLEE YEARS, 1945–1951

Politicians of all political parties have tended to treat the Attlee years with respect, viewing them variously as evidence of the success of planned socialism, of the shift to the Left, or of the working out of Liberal policies forged in the 1930s and the Second World War. Yet if the Attlee years have been the apotheosis of Labour's planned socialist economy for many politicians this is not the view held by many historians. They have been less sympathetic and willing to challenge the mythology which has been built around the events of 1945 to 1951. For some the achievements of the Attlee years, even stripped of the mythology, were impressive (14, ii). For others, usually more Left-wing writers, the Attlee governments had little real purpose or direction (14, i).

Yet it would be harsh judgement which did not at least recognise the lasting achievements of the social-welfare measures introduced during these years. Though such measures were never the prerogative of any one party it is clear that the Labour Party had laid claim to some of the detailed welfare planning before the Second World War with *Labour's Immediate Programme*, in 1937, which was presented to the electorate as *Let Us Face the Future* in 1945. Both documents made reference to the need for a National Health Service, national insurance and a house-building programme.

In a wide sense, the Beveridge Report had provided the context in which the Labour Party was able to press a reluctant Churchill to accept some form of commitment to post-war reconstruction and social welfare. The strongest evidence of the direct influence of the Beveridge Report is the National Insurance Act, which was committed to the principle of providing a 'National Minimum Standard'. There were minor differences from the Beveridge Report, and there was an element of means testing, but to all intents and purposes the Labour Government proved to be a faithful advocate of Beveridge's scheme – of which it was partly the instigator (2).

In contrast, the creation of the National Health Service, which became the plank of the welfare state, owed little to Beveridge. The NHS was largely the product of Aneurin Bevan's initiatives, as has become clear with the recent availability of Cabinet and government records (4, Cabinet, 18 October 1945). Although the Beveridge Report deliberated on the need for a comprehensive health and rehabilitation service and advocated a universal contributory scheme of health provision which would make medical and dental treatment immediately available, whether in private or public health hospitals, it did not envisage the nationalization of the hospitals which Bevan's National Health Service Bill intended, nor the extent to which Bevan's scheme contemplated GPs being drawn into the NHS on a quasi-salaried basis.

The passing of the National Health Service Bill in 1946 and its introduction in 1948 were, of course, accompanied by a tremendous outburst of opposition from the British Medical Association, which held plebiscites of its members to reveal their opposition to what they saw as the loss of professional independence. But in the end Bevan appeased the bulk of the profession (3), and the creation of the NHS was, by any terms, a success. Bevan could rightly stress, with a certain amount of pride, that the 'National Health Service and the Welfare State have come to be used as interchangeable terms. . .'

Once the NHS was introduced, however, it proved to be an enormous financial burden. When the decision to form the NHS was taken in 1946 it was estimated that it would cost £126 million. During its first year, 1948–9, expenditure exceeded £278 million, rising to £356 million between 1950 and 1951. These unexpectedly high figures dismayed Attlee, Cripps and Morrison who, by 1949, were strenuously seeking to force the Minister of Health to reduce expenditure.

As Cabinet and government records now reveal, the conflict first emerged in the autumn of 1949, at a time when the Labour Cabinet had decided to devalue the £ (4, 5, 6, 7). It is clear that Herbert Morrison was strongly advised by his civil servants, particularly E.M. Nicholson, that the truculent attitude of Bevan was leading 'the Government straight for another 1931 crisis in the very near future' (7, i).

As a result, Morrison and the Cabinet began to press for the introduction of prescription charges. However, the timing of the general election of February 1950 helped Bevan to fend off such a move (6, v). But that was only a temporary victory. In January 1951, Bevan was moved from the Ministry of Health to the Ministry of Labour and his old post was excluded from the Cabinet. Marquand, the new Minister of Health, proved more agreeable to the levy of charges on dental and optical services. Marginalized, Bevan's only recourse was to resign from the Cabinet in 1951, in one of the best recorded episodes of the Attlee years, which also saw Harold Wilson and John Freeman leave the Government.

Though the Attlee governments were most famous for the lasting impact they had on the welfare of the nation they are also remembered for the introduction of nationalization, normally referred to at the time as the 'socialization of industry'. Between 1946 and 1948, Labour nationalized the Bank of England, coal mines, electricity, gas and the railways. Thereafter, the pace of change slowed down, much to the dismay of the Labour Left, as Herbert Morrison advocated a policy of 'consolidation'. It looked to the Left as though the Attlee government was baulking on the more controversial aspects of its nationalization, which would be more sternly fought by the employers than were previous moves towards public ownership (12, i). A pusillanimous Labour Cabinet thus faced hostile steel manufacturers, a determined Opposition and an obdurate House of Lords. But, in the end, the industry was formally nationalized in 1950. Yet it was evident that the momentum of public ownership was slowing down and by 1950 the chief concern of the Cabinet appeared to be the need to make every nationalized industry more efficient and effective (12, ii).

Attlee's government also achieved modest, though controversial, success in the field of foreign policy. It attempted to remain even-handed, between the Jews and the Arabs, in its administration of Palestine and recognized that the immediate admission of 100,000 Jews (9, i) would create serious problems with the Arabs. Eventually the continued illegal immigration of the Jews, the episode of the ship *Exodus*, the violence against British troops, the United Nations Committee and its advocacy of the partition into Jewish and Arab states, and the civil war, forced Bevin and the Cabinet to allow the creation of the state of Israel in January 1949 and to arrange the ignominious withdrawal of British troops (9, ii).

In contrast, Britain's withdrawal from India was one of the monumental achievements of the Attlee years. British Labour politicians had been committed to Indian independence before the Second World War – but the problem they faced in Office was reconciling the demands of both Hindus and Moslems. An interim government was formed, under Pandit Nehru, in September 1946. But the rising level of violence between the Hindus and the Moslems threatened its continued existence and provoked the Viceroy, Lord Mountbatten, to bring forward the withdrawal of British troops to 15 August 1947 – the day on which the Indian Congress agreed that India and Pakistan would formally become independent states (10).

It was during these years that Britain's relationship with the rest of the world was more clearly defined. For better or worse, Ernest Bevin, the Foreign Secretary, sedulously sought to get a commitment to the defence of Western Europe, against the threat of Russian invasion, from the United States. At first the USA refused to give such an undertaking. But events moved quickly in 1948. On 5 March 1948 there was the Communist coup in Czechoslovakia, the Russians pressured the President of Finland to visit Moscow and also imposed a blockade on West Berlin in the summer of the same year. The last of these events necessitated the Berlin airlift, which involved American cooperation with the British in order to maintain 'West' Berlin.

By the autumn of 1948, amidst genuine fears that the Western European nations would be overrun by the Russians in the event of war, there were clear signs that a Western Alliance was likely to be formed. By February 1949 the draft of the North Atlantic Pact had been agreed (11). The United States finally agreed to commit itself to the support of the Western European nations at the Washington Conference on 4 April 1949.

Despite its achievements, the first Attlee government was clearly in difficulty by 1950. It had achieved its main legislative thrust in the immediate post-war years, the electorate was less supportive of it in the 1950 General Election (13) and many of its leading figures were gone. Its initiative was stifled further by financial difficulties and the Korean War created problems for its defence budget. In addition the trade union movement was no longer prepared to force its members to accept wage restraint as the consensus between trade unions and government began to erode (8, i, ii). Ever since 1945 the trade unions had accepted the need to sublimate their sectional interests to the needs of a reforming Labour government. Wage restraint had been accepted by the TUC and its member unions generally discouraged strike action. But this arrangement was beginning to break down by the autumn of 1950 and Labour ministers became concerned that the outbreak of strikes in 1950 was promoted by the Communist Party.

It was only a matter of time before Attlee, plagued with domestic and foreign problems, decided to call a general election for October 1951 (14). Though Labour remained the most popular political party it only captured 295 seats compared with the 321 gained by the Conservatives.

Recent writers have been right to attack the political myths which have surrounded the Attlee governments of 1945 to 1951. In no way can it be correct to see these administrations as calmly, and with deliberate intent, introducing the planned socialist state devised by democratic socialists and agreed to by the nation as a whole as some contemporary politicians would have us believe. There was much less planning than the myth allows for and far too much hesitancy. Nevertheless, the Attlee governments did extend public ownership and achieved some notable, if controversial, successes in foreign affairs. Indeed, the successes of the Labour governments should not be overlooked. They offered the most effective evidence of what could be achieved by a democratic socialist administration. They brought about a change of direction of the British nation and moved government to a more humanitarian concern for its people, committing it to the maintenance of full employment – a sharp contrast to the events which followed the First World War. These achievements were considerable and formed the basis of the policies of successive governments, at least until 1979.

1) *C.R. Attlee, Prime Minister, reflecting upon the achievements of the Labour government in introducing the social legislation which helped to create the welfare state between 1945 and 1948*
(D. Houghton, *The Family Circle*)
A new proud chapter has been written in Britain's social history. Since

1945 a series of Acts have been put on the Statute Book which strike at the very roots of poverty and for the first time in our history provide for a minimum standard of living below which no one may fall.

This little book tells the human story of that legislation in a form which I am sure will make a profound impression on all who read it. For this is not merely a chronicle of Acts of Parliament. It is the story of a great victory over those blind economic forces which have for generations been the cause of so much suffering and want among our people, and which were first challenged on the floor of the House of Commons by Keir Hardie, and later in the remarkable works of Sydney and Beatrice Webb on the Poor Law.

Today the inspired dreams of our pioneers of social justice have been translated into the most advanced social legislation to be found in any part of the world, and I commend this book to all who have the cause of true freedom at heart. No more fitting testament to the power and determination of Britain's people, despite all adversities, could have been written.

2) *The Social Legislation introduced by the Labour Government between 1945 and 1948*
(D. Houghton, *The Family Circle*, pp.11, 13, 23, 26)
The Beveridge Report, in recommending a scheme of Family Allowances, said that although real wages had increased by a third in the last thirty years, want had not been abolished. This was due in part to the fact that wages alone were not enough to support the larger families.

The Family Allowance Act was passed by the Coalition Government and brought into operation by the Labour Government in August 1946.

The Family Allowance is 5s. a week for each child *after the first*. This is paid out of taxation and not out of the contributions we pay under the insurance scheme. [. . .]

The Labour Government's National Insurance Scheme is a better-than-Beveridge plan – and better than the Coalition Government's plan.

We received a big instalment of the new scheme when in October 1946, the Labour Government increased existing pensions from 20s. to 42s. for a married couple, and from 10s. to 26s. for a single person. Over three million old-age and widowed pensioners benefited from that increase. The higher standard pension *reduced by a million* the number of folk who had previously sought extra help from the Assistance Board. [. . .]

The scheme provides for each insurance class, benefits suited to their way of life.

Class 1, the *employed*, no matter what their position or pay, are entitled to *all* benefits.

Class 2, *the man (or woman) in business on his own*, is *not* insured for *unemployment benefit* or for *industrial injuries benefits*; the risk of unemployment to a man (or woman) working on his own account, and the risk of injury at his work, were not considered to be risks against which the State need insure him; but he *is* insured for *sickness*.

Class 3, *the man (or woman) who is not in any kind of paid employment*; it follows that people in this class are not entitled to any of the worker's benefits. Therefore a man or women doing no paid work is *not* able to claim (a) *unemployment*, (b) *sickness* or (c) *industrial injuries benefits*. A woman doing no paid work has *no claim* to maternity allowances. This is paid only to women in jobs or in business, to make up for loss of *earnings*. [. . .]

For more than three centuries the Poor Law has imposed on local ratepayers the duty of relieving the 'needy poor', old and young, who look in vain for help from other sources.

The National Assistance Act makes this a *nation-wide* instead of a local charge, and transfers that work to the new National Assistance Board, a central body working to a single co-ordinated plan through its own local officers.

National Assistance replaces existing schemes for the assistance of the aged and infirm, the sick, and the unemployed, who are unable to get help, or enough help from elsewhere.

In particular, the Act transfers from the local authorities to the National Assistance Board:

(a) the responsibility for giving money help to the blind;
(b) the special allowances to certain persons suffering from pulmonary tuberculosis who give up work to have treatment; and
(c) outdoor relief to those in need.
[. . .]

The Labour Government has abolished doctors' bills. From 5 July, no medical, surgical, or dental treatment depends on whether we can afford it. The National Health Service has emancipated the sick.

The Beveridge Report said that sickness insurance for all should be linked with a complete medical service for all. [. . .]
[. . .] The principle is that whatever we need for health, or in sickness, we get – if it is there to be had. [. . .]

Everyone of us is covered by the National Health Service – literally everybody. Man, woman, and child; old and young; married or single; rich or poor; *everybody* in Great Britain.

3) *Aneurin Bevan on the 'Free Health Service'*
(A. Bevan, *In Place of Fear*, pp.75–6, 79, 81, 86–7)

When I was engaged in formulating the main principles of the British Health Service, I had to give careful study to various proposals for financing it, and as this aspect of the scheme is a matter of anxious discussion in many other parts of the world, it may be useful if I set down the main considerations that guided my choice. In the first place, what was to be its financial relationship with National Insurance; should the Health Service be on an insurance basis? I decided against this. It had always seemed to me that a personal contributory basis was peculiarly inappropriate to a National Health Service. There is, for example, the question of the qualifying period. That is to say, so many contributions for this benefit, and so many more for additional benefits, until enough contributions are eventually paid to qualify the contributor for the full range of benefits.

In the case of health treatment this would give rise to endless anomalies, quite apart from the administrative jungle which would be created. This is already the case in countries where people insure privately for operations as distinct from hospital or vice versa. Whatever may be said for it in private insurance, it would be out of place in a national scheme. Imagine a patient lying in hospital after an operation and ruefully reflecting that if the operation had been delayed another month he would have qualified for the operation benefit. Limited benefits for limited contributions ignore the overriding consideration that the full range of health machinery must be there in any case, independent of the patient's right of access to it. [. . .]

One thing the community cannot do is insure against itself. What it can and must do is to set aside an agreed proportion of the national revenues for the creation and maintenance of the service it has pledged itself to provide. This is not so much insurance as a prudent policy of capital investment. [. . .]

The means of collecting the revenues for the health service are already in the possession of most modern states, and that is the normal system of taxation.

This was the course which commended itself to me and it is the basis of the finances of the British Health Service. Its revenues are provided by the Exchequer in the same way as other forms of public expenditure. I am afraid this is not yet fully understood. Many people still think they pay for the National Health Service by way of their contribution to the National Insurance Scheme. The confusion arose because the new service sounded so much like the old National Health Insurance, and it was launched on the same date as the National Insurance Scheme. [. . .]

The National Health Service and the Welfare State have come to be used as interchangeable terms, and in the mouths of some people as terms of reproach. Why this is so it is not difficult to understand, if you view everything from the angle of a strictly individualistic Competitive Society. A free health service is pure Socialism and as such it is opposed to the hedonism of capitalist society. To call it something for nothing is absurd because everything has to be paid for in some way or another. [. . .]

But the hardest task for any public representative charged with the duty of making a free Health Service available to the community, is overcoming the fears, real and imaginary, of the medical profession. [. . .]

. . . it was with the B.M.A. I had to negotiate. [. . .]

I enjoyed the challenge. My trade union experience had taught me to distinguish between the atmosphere of the mass demonstration and the quite different mood of the negotiating table. [. . .] Also it was easy for me to enable them to win victories, for they usually worked themselves up into a fever of protest against proposals which had never been made. Thus they would "never be made into civil servants". As I never intended they should, I was able to concede the point without difficulty.

Then there must be "free choice of doctor". I myself was most anxious to insist on this, for I saw in it one of the most important safeguards for the public. The right of the patient to leave his doctor and choose another whenever he liked, had a double edge that the B.M.A. spokesman did not fully appreciate until later. Then there was the demand for full rights of free expression of opinion, both about the Health Service and anything else. To this again I was most ready to respond, as it had never occurred to me that anything otherwise had been intended.

4) *Extracts from the Cabinet Conclusions, mainly relating to the issues of the National Health Service and cuts in expenditure on health c. 1945 –51* (Cab. 128 series, PRO)
Cab. 39 (45), 9 October 1945.
Minister of Health stated [on housing policy] 'that the bulk of work would have to be done through the local authorities'. A high proportion of the houses built between the two wars had been built by private enterprise for sale: the bulk of the houses to be built in the next few years should be built by local authorities for letting. There would be a strong campaign for relaxing controls so as to give further scope for house building by private enterprise, but such a course would, in his view, lead to administrative chaos and inflated costs.
Cab. 40 (45), 11 October 1945.
Minister of Health revealed White Paper on N.H. Service (Cmnd 6502), proposing to leave voluntary hospitals under their own independent management.
Cab. 43 (45), 18 October 1945.
The Lord President of the Council said that while he fully appreciated the attractions of a logical and clear-cut scheme of the kind proposed by the Minister of Health he felt that before accepting the Minister's proposal, the Cabinet ought to consider fully whether the opposition which they would arouse . . . did not outway the arguments based on grounds of administrative convenience and technical efficiency. It would be unwise to underrate the pride which local people took in their hospitals, whether voluntary or municipal, and he feared that the Minister's scheme, for which there was no authority in the Party Programme and which involved a departure from the terms of a resolution passed at the last annual Party Conference, would arouse such a stir of opposition as to jeopardize the passage of the National Health Service Bill in the current Session. The Government was

virtually committed to schemes for the nationalisation of electricity, gas and transport services which would mean the transfer of important functions from local authorities.

[. . .] If, in addition, they were to lose the hospital services and possibly other health services (eg. the maternity and child welfare clinics, the school medical services), the fabric of local government could be dangerously weakened. [. . .]

The Minister of Health said that he had considered very carefully the points made by the Lord President of the Council, but that he still felt that the only way to make the hospital services efficient was to centralise responsibility for them. Since it was impossible to leave the situation as it was, and since any change would involve controversy, was it not better for Government to propose the scheme which would give the most efficient service and could best be defended on merits? He did not believe that a satisfactory service could be run under a system of joint committees which would have to obtain their funds by precepting on local authorities for varying resources.

Cab.10 (50), 13 March 1950.

Minister of Health (stated that) in an expanding service at an early stage of its development it was inevitable that expenditure should increase and that some of the increase should be reflected in Supplementary Estimates. In present circumstances he could not favour the imposition of any rigid ceiling on expenditure in 1950–51.

[. . .]

Chancellor of Exchequer (argued strongly that) the Government were determined to enforce effective control on behalf of the responsible Minister in the various stages of hospital expenditure. [. . .]

Cabinet agreed . . .

(2) Agreed to resume at a later date that discussion of the finance of the National Health Service.

Cab. 11 (50), 16 March 1950.

Minister of Health said with reference to the minutes of the Cabinet meeting of 13th March that he had not understood that the Cabinet decided to resume this discussion of the finance of the National Health Service.

Cab. 17 (50), 3 April 1950.

Chancellor of the Exchequer announced a £392 million estimate for

NHS. Limit set. Suggested that the service should not exceed £350 million. Charges on some part of the service.

Minister of Health ... The Government's abandonment of the principle of free and comprehensive health service would be a shock to their supporters in this country and a grave disappointment of Socialist opinion throughout the world. The Government had so far had experience of only one full year's working of the existing system, and he strongly urged that they should not abandon the principle of a free service on the basis of so short a period.

Cab. 18 (50), 4 April 1950.

[At this meeting it was decided to examine the need for NHS cuts and charges for prescriptions and some medical appliances. The Chancellor of the Exchequer and the Health Minister undertook to examine means of introducing stricter controls over health expenditure.]

On the other hand, doubts were expressed about the wisdom of the Government's making an early announcement of their intention to take power to impose charges before they had been able to announce what service charges should be imposed, what the scale of charges would be and what classes of person might be excluded.

Cab. 25 (51), 9 April 1951, 10.30 am.

Minister of Labour [now A. Bevan] said he had always been opposed to the introduction of charges for dentures and spectacles.

Cab. 30 (51), 23 April 1951.

[Ministers discussed the National Health Service Bill.]

It had not been found possible to find a form of words which would satisfy the Minister of Labour, and he now resigned from the Government.

Cab. 31 (51), 26 April 1951.

Minister of Health [now R.A. Marquand, had announced that] charges for dentures and spectacles would be in operation on 13/4/51, and revenue for charge estimated at £12.5 million. But as soon as Government announced intention, demand increased. In the last few days applications for dentures had doubled and demand for spectacles had risen 25 per cent. Longer the delay in Bill (NHS Bill) the greater would be the loss of revenue.

Patients to bear ½ cost of spectacles and dentures. Charges should not be increased without the authority of a future Parliament.

Cab. 32 (51), 30 April 1950.

Chancellor of Exchequer feels that increase in health charges should be possible without fresh legislation.

5) *The Cabinet 128 Series also provides more detailed minutes of some of the crucial debates connected with health matters*
(Cab. 128/21, PRO)
CM (51) 25th Conclusion, Minute 2   No circulation Record
9 April 1951 – 10.30 am.
Cabinet decision of 22nd March – expenditure on N.H.S. subject to an upper limit of £400 millions. Before decision taken estimate of expenditure for financial year 1951/2 £423 million.
Minister of Labour [Bevan] said he had always been opposed to the introduction of charges for dentures and spectacles. In a Budget of over £4,000 million it should not be difficult to find so small a sum as £13 million.
Minister of Labour and President of the Board of Trade [Harold Wilson] felt that Government would find great difficulty in persuading supporters in the House of Commons to accept this departure from the principle of a free Health Service. [. . .]
Several Ministers expressed the view that, if the Minister of Labour resigned from the Government on this issue, an acute political crisis would develop. With the present Parliamentary majority the Government could not afford any diminution in their voting strength in the House of Commons. And, if the Government fell, as a result of divided counsel within the Cabinet, the Labour Party's prospects at the following General Election would be greatly prejudiced.
CM (51) 26th Conclusion 9 April 1951, 6.30 pm.
Minister of Labour [Bevan] said he had seen PM before 22 March and had made it clear that he would not be able to share collective responsibility for a decision to abandon the conception of a free Health Service. This was, for him, a question of principle. He had given five years to building up the Health Service: he had proclaimed it on many public platforms as one of the outstanding achievements of the Labour Party in office; he had, in particular, upheld the conception of a free Service as the embodiment of Socialist principles. It was too much now to ask him now to go into the discussion lobby in support of a measure authorising the imposition of charges for dentures and spectacles provided under this Service. [. . .] But latterly, he had come to feel that

he could bring more influence to bear on Government policy from outside the Cabinet than he could ever hope to exercise within it, and, when a Minister reached that position, it was time for him to go. President of the Board of Trade [Harold Wilson] . . . He now wished to make it clear that, if the Cabinet maintained their decision to introduce these charges, he would feel unable to share collective responsibility for that decision and, like the Minister of Labour, would feel obliged to resign from the Government.

[. . .] Minister of Labour pointed out that if he resigned from the Government he would also express his opposition to the economic consequences of the increased defence programme. [. . .]

Minister of Labour resigned from Government.

6) *Correspondence from the office of the Lord President of the Council (Herbert Morrison), on the issue of National Health Service cuts* (Cab 124, folio 1187, PRO)

(i)   *The Times*, 26 September 1949

Mr. Bevan, Minister of Health, speaking at a rally at Hednesfod, Staffordshire last night. . . 'I have made up my mind that the National Health Service is not going to be touched, and there is no disposition by the Government to touch it' he said. 'The Government have made up their mind to solve the problems without reducing the social services, and the health service is sacrosanct.

The Telegraph, 7 October 1949

Mr. Bevan, Minister of Health, said yesterday that the Government had set their faces against a Health Tax, if what was meant was a payment made by a patient at the moment he needed treatment. Mr. Bevan was holding his first press conference for three years.

(ii) *Letter from A. Bevan to Stafford Cripps, Chancellor of the Exchequer, dated 9 December 1949, responding to Cripps's suggestion for cuts in health expenditure in a letter 28 November 1949*

My dear Stafford

I have been looking very carefully at your letter of 28th November about further economies in the health service. [. . .]

[. . .] I think that a proposal to charge two or three shillings for some 40 per cent of 'prescriptions' would give rise to a lot of surprise, resentment, and in many cases hardship.

Finally, my general comment on our method of approaching cuts in the health service. I am sure that this piecemeal method, of taking away a little benefit here or a little benefit there, or of importing charges into the service for one item but not for another comparable item, is thoroughly wrong in that it puts us in the vulnerable position of discarding some of our earlier promises and going back on some of the big principles of the scheme without any real compensating advantage. I think we must see the problem clearly and make up our minds; either we must stand to the health service as a whole, sticking to all principles on which we founded it, or else we should clearly admit that – much as we still believe that it was, and is, the right service to aim at – our economic position renders it impossible to have it for some years to come; in the latter event, we leave it on the statute book for the future but in the meantime substitute a revised, interim and austerity service until times are better – this interim service being worked out on different principles and after an intensive revision of the whole field. I personally should regret the latter, as you know. But I should infinitely prefer to tackle it that way, if finally it proved essential, than to go on with a process of whittling away which brings small savings coupled with large discredit in many people's eyes. What do you think about this?

(iii) *Letter of E.M. Nicholson, adviser, to the Lord President of the Council, 18 January 1950*

[...] It is very unsatisfactory that the Minister of Health should have missed the opportunity to get to this stage by the end of November, in which case it might be coming into force next month. Moreover the scheme, apparently unavoidably, promised a yield of not more than £6 million against the £10 million estimated by the Minister originally. Either, therefore, the total economies will be whittled down by this amount, or the Minister will have to make economies of £4 million in some other way, or one of his colleagues will have to shoulder the burden for him.

If the Committee accept the scheme the Health Minister ought to report to the Prime Minister (or to the Chancellor of the Exchequer) the expected short fall, and give their proposals for making it good. Some of it might, with advantage, be saved by energetic steps to economies over the merit and distinction award to specialists for example . . .

(iv) *Extracts from a letter from the Chancellor of the Exchequer to the Prime Minister (R. Stafford Cripps to Clem Attlee), 3 February 1950* [The letter concentrated upon the cost of the NHS and the need for cuts in expenditure.]

Increases in the scale of the original estimates makes ordinary budgeting impossible. They reduce the budget to nonsense.

With an Election imminent . . . it is not possible to consider remedial measures in the immediate future. It is, however, plain that as soon as the Election is over, the future of the service will have to receive immediate consideration and that serious and difficult issue will arise.

I think that you and my senior colleagues should be aware of this situation now so that it will be in mind from the outset after Election.

I have sent a copy of this minute to the Lord President and (of course) to the Minister of Health and Secretary of State for Scotland.

(v) *Letter from A. Bevan to C. Attlee, the Prime Minister,* 2 February 1950

My dear Clem,

You have, no doubt, noted that at the last meeting of the Lord President's Committee it was decided in my absence (unfortunately, I had a slight cold and could not attend) that I should at once proceed with discussions with chemists and doctors about the arrangements for charging a shilling for prescriptions, despite the fact that because of exceptions the saving will now be no more than £5 millions.

I have submitted a paper to the Cabinet but it was not possible to discuss it on Tuesday. As you no doubt know, I am now leaving London on a long speaking tour for the Party, and then must visit my own constituency.

I am therefore, instructing my office not to proceed with any discussions until after the Election. This will not prejudice a final decision on the question of making a change, but I am sure that you will appreciate that to start discussions with the British Medical Association, including Charles Hill, who is a Conservative candidate for Luton, would be the height of folly, for our proposals would be certain to become known and would lend themselves to grotesque misrepresentation by the Opposition.

We shall not, in fact, lose anything by this procedure since I have just given a pledge that the Regulations would not come into force until Parliament had had an opportunity of discussing them. I hope, therefore, that you will agree with the line which I have adopted.

7) *Further Correspondence from the office of the Lord President on the issue of the National Health Service Cuts*
(Cab. 124, folio 1188, PRO)

(i) *Letter from E.M. Nicholson to the Lord President, 11 March 1950*
[. . .] It ought, however, to be emphasised that however much the Minister of Health can say on the virtues and merits of vast expenditure on the sick he is heading the Government straight for another 1931 financial crisis in the very near future, and unless the Government can show that it knows how to adopt a pace of development of the Health Service which the national economy can bear something will have to go before long.

Probably the best approach would be for the Cabinet to set a ceiling figure on the National Health Service as on the Defence Service . . . [Discusses a ceiling of £300 million and thus the need for £93 million cuts on present estimates.] This would still give the Health Service well over double the figure (£126 million) on the basis of which the Government decided to go forward with the Service in 1946.

(ii) *Circular from E.M. Nicholson and addressed to the Lord President, 17 March 1950*
[Nicholson outlined the problem that the Minister of Health saw no way in which he could bring about significant reductions in expenditure. He suggested that expansion could be allowed unfettered, the Government could impose an arbitrary ceiling on expenditure, that the principle of a free service would have to be modified, or that some other means of installing financial

responsibility would have to devized. He then outlined the wisdom of the alternatives.]

We are left face to face with the basic problem that the Government had, in effect, signed a blank cheque to meet a general public demand, the scale and composition of which is entirely unknown. . . Therefore, there seems no escape from some sort of ceiling allowance for Health, . . .

(iii) *Letter from Herbert Morrison to Sir Norman Brook, 17 April 1950*
I note from your minute of 14 April that the Prime Minister would like to have my help on the Committee to keep the cost of the National Health Service under review. I feel that the present grave difficulties in connection with the National Health Service would not have arisen had matters been brought to the appropriate Ministerial Committees as they should have been before action was taken or expenditure authorised. Before agreeing to serve I would like to be satisfied that the scope and terms of reference of the Committee will be such as to ensure that all policies behind expenditure, and of new developments involving expenditure, are first submitted to the Committee by the Health Minister after discussion with the Treasury and before any action is taken.

I would also like to be satisfied that the scope of the Committee will include the fixing of a ceiling figure for the national resources to be made available to the National Health Service.

8) *Industrial Relations and the Labour Governments, 1945–1951*
(Cab 124, folio 1194, PRO)
(i) *Draft of a Broadcast by the Minister of Labour, not dated but given in 1950 and raising the issue of the Communist threat in British industrial relations*
In March last the Communists held a National Industrial Conference in pursuance of their publically declared policy of concentrating their activities on industry. [*The Times*, 6 March recorded Harry Pollitt, General Secretary of the Communist Party, as stating that] '. . . the great issues would be settled not in the area of the reactionary Parliament, but by workers mass struggles in the factories and streets.' [The Minister went on to

discuss the difficulties of imposing legislation if trade unions were to pursue their legitimate activities but added that] What I am referring to is the unofficial activity which is now clearly being followed as part of a deliberate plan. In the last year or two, we have had experience of a number of unofficial strikes ... [The Minister then mentioned the British Dock Strike of 1949 and other strikes as evidence of Communist Party activity to incite industrial unrest.] The President of the Amalgamated Society of Woodworkers earlier this week stated that 'The use of the strike weapon by irresponsible agent provacateurs must be seriously curtailed.' No doubt, I shall be told there is a need for militancy in the Movement to stem the power of the employers, and that this is the object of the unofficial committees, and to weaken the authority of the officials. It sounds quite friendly, does it not. But I am not greatly enamoured of people who stab me in the back, even in a friendly spirit.

(ii) *Letter to the Prime Minister in October 1950, from P. Jordan, about the dangers of the Gas Strike*
[This strike had continued for two weeks and there was rising concern about the lack of Government intervention and the involvement of the Communist Party.]

It is argued that, under a Socialist Government, the power of the Trade Unions to hold the loyalty of their members must inevitably wither, because the Unions are so completely connected with the government that they must attempt the impossible task of running with the hare and hunting with the hounds. The argument concludes that so long as wage restraint is necessary unofficial strikes will become more numerous, because men and women who are mainly preoccupied with their immediate living conditions will lose faith in a leadership that must now take account of interests far wider than they were elected to serve.
[It was then argued that legal action against the gas strikers might speed up that loss of respect of trade unions and the TUC by the workers.]

9) *The Labour Government and Palestine*
(Cab. 128, Cabinet Conclusions, PRO)

(i) *Cabinet Meeting, 4 October 1945*

The Prime Minister said that since the memoranda were circulated there had been a marked increase in the agitation in the question in the United States, where our difficulties with regard to the immediate problem of immigration into Palestine were not clearly understood. [. . .]

In discussion stress was laid on the importance of making a full statement of the facts of the situation. The admission of 100,000 Jews to Palestine, while it would lead to an explosion in the Middle East would not solve the problem of Jews in Europe. The same opportunity should be taken for correcting the impression that all the Jews in Europe were still living in intolerable conditions.

(ii) *Cabinet Meeting, 11 November 1947*

2. The Cabinet were informed that the Defence Committee had been considering, with the Chiefs of Staff, what was the earliest date by which it would be practicable to complete the withdrawal of the British administration and Armed Forces of Palestine. The Defence Committee were satisfied that it would be practicable to complete the withdrawal by 1 August 1948; and it now proposed to authorise the United Kingdom representative at the United Nations to make an announcement to this effect at an appropriate stage in the discussions of the Palestine Committee in order to dispel any remaining uncertainty about the sincerity of our intentions.

The Cabinet:

(1) Took note of the Defence Committee's conclusion that it would be practicable to complete by 1st April 1948, the withdrawal of the British administration and Armed Forces from Palestine.

(2) Invited the Foreign Secretary to reconsider the form and timing of the announcement to this effect, in the light of the latest developments in the discussions on Palestine at the United Nations; and took note that the text of the instructions to be sent to the United Kingdom representative at the United Nations would be settled in consultation between the Prime Minister, the

Foreign Secretary, the Minister of Defence and the Secretary of State for the Colonies.

10) *The Labour Government and India, 1947*
(PRO, Cab. 128, Cabinet Conclusions)
Cabinet Meeting, 23 May 1947
[. . .] The refusal of the Muslim League to participate in the work of the Constituent Assembly had destroyed any possibility that the Cabinet Mission plan could be successfully put into effect. The League had, indeed, entered the Interim Government, but the failure of both Parties to co-operate within that Government made it improbable that it could continue to hold together for much longer. The extensive discussions which Lord Mountbatten had had with the various political leaders since he arrived in India had convinced him that there was no prospect of a Union of India either on the basis of the Cabinet Mission plan or any other basis, and further that, unless a very early announcement was made of the method by which His Majesty's Government intended to transfer power, widespread communal disturbance would be inevitable. All the Indian Parties were now convinced that, in view of the recalcitrant attitude of the Muslim League, some form of partition was to be conceded, it was a necessary corollory that there should also be a division of Bengal and the Punjab.

The Viceroy had convened a conference of Indian leaders for 2nd June, at which he would make a final effort to secure agreement on the basis of the Cabinet Mission's plan. [. . .]

The Prime Minister drew attention to the difficulties and dangers necessarily inherent in any scheme of partition. The situation in many parts of India was already highly inflammable. In the Punjab, in particular, the proposed announcement was likely in the Governor's view to provoke serious disorder and bloodshed. [. . .] But whatever the practical difficulties involved, there appeared to be no alternative to partition.

11) *The North Atlantic Pact: the formation of the North Atlantic Treaty Organisation, 1949*
(PRO, Cab 129, CP (49) 56. This document was presented to the Cabinet on 22 February, CM 14 (49). The text of the treaty was approved by the Cabinet, which recorded its congratulations to Bevin on 10 March 1949)

THE NORTH ATLANTIC PACT
Memorandum by the Secretary of State
for Foreign Affairs

[. . .]

Recommendation

I recommend that the Cabinet approves the text of the North Atlantic Pact and authorise me to inform the other Government's concerned that His Majesty's Government are willing to sign it.

Observation

My colleagues will observe that Article 5 (mutual assistance), which is the key article of the Treaty, has emerged in a form which can be regarded as very satisfactory. Notwithstanding the doubts and fears caused by the Senate debate of 14 February, the Senate leaders have accepted a wording which retains the conception that an attack on one of the parties is an attack on all, as well as making clear that the measures which the signatories are bound to take in the face of such an attack include 'the use of armed force'. We would have preferred to see the words 'as it deems necessary' read 'as may be necessary', but the Senatorial leaders were unwilling to give way on this. We have, however, succeeded in eliminating from this Article any reference to 'constitutional processes', though we were not able to avoid this idea appearing elsewhere in the Treaty (Article 11). [. . .]

On the whole we can be satisfied with the results of the long negotiations which have taken place over this text; the Pact has teeth in it and will give strong grounds for encouragement to Europe.

At the same time it is a strictly defensive pact and in harmony with the Charter of the United Nations. Its object is to reinforce but not to replace the security provided by the Charter. [. . .]

12) *Nationalisation, or the 'Socialization of Industry'.*

[The nationalization programme embraced the Bank of England (May 1946) the coal mines (January 1947), electricity (April 1948), gas (May 1948) and the railways (May 1948). The Conservatives put up little more than token opposition to these measures, since many of them were ailing and of little value to their owners. But there was more determined opposition to attempt to nationalize the iron and steel industry and by the late 1940s Herbert Morrison, Lord President of the Council and the great initiator of public ownership schemes was attempting to water down iron and steel nationalization and appeared less than fully committed to further nationalization or 'socialization of industry'.]

(i) *Iron and Steel Nationalization*

(PRO, Cab. 128, Cab. 6 (50) 4, Cabinet Meeting 2 March 1950)
     Iron and Steel Act

The Minister of Supply recalled that under the terms of the Act the Iron and Steel Corporation could not be appointed until 1 October, 1950, and the vesting dates to be presented by a Ministerial order which would not be subject to any Parliamentary proceedings – could not be earlier than 1st January, 1951. Thus, no formal steps to bring the Act into operation could be taken before 1 October. The Minister said that, if the Government had been returned with a larger majority, he would have appointed an informal organising committee to undertake the preparatory work which ought to be done before the Corporation was formally constituted; but he had not announced his intention to appoint such a committee and in the present circumstances he would not propose to appoint one. . . .

The Minister of Health said that, by the terms of the statement made by the Minister of Supply in the House of Commons on 16 November . . . the Government became free immediately after the Election to approach individuals who might serve as members of the Corporation . . . He also favoured a public announcement to the effect that the Government intended to go forward with their preparatory steps. If they showed any signs of hesitancy in this matter, the confidence of their supporters would be undermined and the Opposition would be encouraged to press for an assurance that no further steps would be taken towards the implementation of the Act until after the next General Election.

Other Ministers took the view that it would be unrealistic to suppose that in the present circumstances [Labour's narrow victory in the 1950 General Election] the leaders of the steel industry would co-operate with the Government in preparing to bring the Act into operation, and that the Minister of Supply would be courting a rebuff if he tried to begin these informal preparations at the present stage.

(ii) *Socialized Industries*
(PRO, Cab. 128, Cab. 18 (50), 4 April 1950)

The Lord President explained that his memorandum was the result of long consideration of this subject by the Socialization of Industries Committee and of two meetings which the Committee had held with the chairman of the boards of socialized industries. The boards and the responsible ministers had affected with great success the transition from private to public ownership. It was now, however, necessary to consider whether the arrangements for checking the efficiency of these industries was adequate, and how the growing demand for parliamentary control should be met. If Parliament and the public felt that there was no check on the efficient working of each socialized industry, other than the opinion of the responsible Minister and the board, there would be strong pressure for the appointment of a Select Committee. He and his colleagues on the Socialization of Industries Committee were therefore induced to favour the setting up of an efficiency unit for the socialized industries.

13) *1950 General Election*
(PRO, Cab 128, Cab 5 (50), 25 February 1950)
[Labour was returned to Office with its parliamentary representation reduced to 315, compared to 393 in 1945. It was a narrow majority which threatened to prevent the Labour Government introducing its programme, including the nationalization of the iron and steel industry.]
The Cabinet met to consider the situation resulting from the General Election. With six returns still outstanding, 314 seats had been won by Labour, 294 by Conservatives and their supporters, 8 by Liberals and 2 by Irish Nationalists. The remaining seat was the Speaker's. Thus whatever the results in the six outstanding constituencies, Labour would have a majority over all other Parties in the new House of Commons.

The Prime Minister said that the King's Government must be carried on and, as Labour would have a majority, the proper course was for a Labour administration to remain in office. It must, however, be recognised that, with so small a majority, there would be great difficulty in transacting Government business in the House of Commons. There could, in particular, be no question of attempting to carry through any of the major controversial legislation which had been promised in the Party's Election Manifesto. Very careful consideration would also have to be given to the content and presentation of the Budget.

14) *1951 General Election*
(*Manchester Guardian*, 8 October 1951)

[The October 1951 General Election saw the defeat of the Labour Party – the 14 million votes it received, the highest ever won by any party up to that time, was only sufficient to return 295 MPs. Thus the Conservative Party took Office under the leadership of Winston Churchill. Nevertheless, there was great respect for the way in which Attlee, and the Labour Party, had conducted itself.]

Mr. Churchill described the campaign of 1950 as 'demure'. That of 1951 is so far no less decorous and restrained. That it is so is due in no small measure to the Prime Minister. . . He has never cheapened himself or his argument to gain applause. He has just been his quiet, assured self. What he says may often exasperate but the way he says it is without offence. Even when he appeals to sentiment he makes it hardly distinguishable from an appeal to reason. . . He paints too bright a picture, of course. He avoids, for reasons which though plausible are also convenient, the more difficult topics. There is astonishingly little in his speeches about what his Government will do if re-elected. He might even be held to be damping down the natural enthusiasm that rises up at election times. Yet it is an admirable exhibition of one of the supreme arts of politics, the enhancement of personal respect. And, since electioneering in Britain seems to have become so eminently dull and respectable Mr. Attlee's technique fits the mood perfectly.

15) *Contrasting views of the Attlee Years*
(i)   (J. Hinton, *Labour and Socialism: A History of the British Labour Movement 1867–1974*, p.178)

In 1951 a senior civil servant summed up the record of the Attlee Government: '. . . it puts me in mind of nothing so much as the voyage of Columbus in 1492. You will recall that when Columbus set out he didn't know where he was going; when he arrived he didn't know where he was; and when he returned he didn't known where he had been.' Much of the history of the Labour Party during the next ten years revolved around attempts to make sense of the record of the Attlee Government. Not the least of Labour's problems was to understand why it was that the Conservatives, most unexpectedly, proved to be both ready and able to run the new social order bequeathed to them from the upheavals of the 1940s.

(ii) (K.O. Morgan, *Labour in Power 1945–1951*, pp.502–3)

In the years 1945–51, everything suddenly worked, and with remarkably little difficulty. A number of different factors gave the Labour movement a purpose and united quality it had never possessed before, or perhaps showed again. There was the existence of a powerful respected, experienced group of dominant leaders, Attlee, Bevin, Morrison, Dalton, Cripps, whose authority was almost unquestioned. There was the unifying influence of the war years with their drive for social equality and radical reform. There was the uniquely close relationship between the major unions and the political leadership at all levels of the party. [. . .] The Attlee government was thus unique in its structural cohesiveness and in its legislative vitality. [. . .] It was without doubt the most effective of all Labour governments, perhaps amongst the most effective of any British government since the passage of the 1832 Reform Act. . . It brought the British Labour movement to the zenith of its achievement as a political instrument of humanitarian reform. But it did so by evading, rather than resolving, those dilemmas inherent in the potent, beguiling vision of socialism in our time.

BIBLIOGRAPHY

PRIMARY SOURCES

Bevan, A., *In Place of Fear*, Heinemann, 1952.

Bradford Observer

Bradford Pioneer

Bradford Typographical Society, Minutes, J.B. Priestley Library, University of Bradford.

Cabinet Conclusions, Cab. 124, Cab. 128, Cab. 23, and other material, PRO.

City of Leeds Labour Party, Minutes, Archives Department, Leeds.

Clarion

Clayton, J., *Why I Joined the Independent Labour Party, Some Plain Statements*, ILP, 1894 or 1895.

Echo

Gladstone Papers, British Museum.

Glasier Papers, University of Liverpool, Archives.

Grayson, Victor, *The Destiny of the Mob*, Worker Press, Huddersfield, c.1908.

Hansard

Houghton, D., *The Family Circle*, Labour Party, 1948.

Independent Labour Party, *Annual Reports*.

ILP News.

ILP Archives, Francis Johnson Collection.

ILP Pamphlets, reproduced by Harvester Press.

Jones, Thomas, *Whitehall Diaries*, I, Oxford University Press, 1969.

Labour Party, *Annual Reports*.

Labour Party Archives, Walworth Road, London.

Labour Party, *Let Us Face the Future*, (London, 1945).

Labour Party, NEC Minutes.

Labour Representation Committee pamphlets.

Labour Representation Committee, Correspondence.

Labour Representation Committee, Leaflets.

Leeds Weekly Citizen

Lister, John, 'The ILP in Halifax', unpublished mss, Calderdale Archives.

Lister, John, Collection, Calderdale Archives.

MacDonald Diaries, MacDonald Collection, PRO.

Manchester Guardian

Mann, Tom, *Memoirs*, (Labour Publishing Co., London, 1923).

National Council of British Socialist Sunday Schools, *Socialist Sunday Schools: Aims, Objectives and Organisation*, (London, pre-1914).

Right to Work National Council, *The Right to Work Manifesto*, Twentieth Century Press, 1908.

Snowden, Philip, *The Individual Under Socialism*, ILP, 1902.

Snowden, Philip, *The Christ that is to be*, ILP, 1903.

Snowden, Philip, *A Plea for Peace*, (Blackburn Labour Party, 1916).

Snowden, Philip, *War or Peace*, National Labour Press, 1918.

Snowden, Philip, *The Big Business Budget*, (Labour Party & TUC, London, 1923).

Snowden, Philip, *The Housewife's Budget*, Labour Party, 1924.

Snowden, Philip, *An Autobiography*, vols. I & II, Ivor Nicholson & Watson, 1934.

Social Democratic Federation, Archives, British Library of Political and Economic Science.

Socialist Review

Socialist Sunday Schools, Aims, Objects and Organisation, Socialist Sunday School Union, 1914.

Stansky, P., ed., *The Left and War: The British Labour Party and World War I*, Oxford University Press, 1969.

The Labour Journal

The Record

The Times

Thompson, W., *Victor Grayson MP*, Worker Press, Huddersfield, 1910.

Tillett, Ben., *Is the Parliamentary Labour Party a failure*, 1908.

G. H. Wood Collection, The Polytechnic Library, Huddersfield.

Yorkshire Factory Times

Yorkshire Post

SECONDARY SOURCES

Addison, Paul, *The Road to 1945: British Politics and the Second World War*, Jonathan Cape, 1975.

Adelman, Paul, *The Rise of the Labour Party 1880–1945*, Longman, 1972.

Barker, Bernard, 'Anatomy of Reform', *International Review of Social History*, xviii, 1973.

Bealey, F., 'Negotiations between the Liberal Party and the Labour Representation Committee before the general election of 1906', *Bulletin of the Institute of Historical Research*, Vol 29/30, 1956/7.

Bealey, Frank and Pelling, Henry, *Labour and Politics, 1900–1906*, Oxford University Press, 1958.

Berkeley, Humphrey, *The Myth that will not die*, Croom Helm, 1978.

Blatchford, Robert, *Merrie England*, Clarion, 1895.

Brockway, A.F., *Socialism over Sixty Years: The Life of Jowett of Bradford* (Allen & Unwin, London, 1946).

Brown, K.D., ed., *The First Labour Party, 1906–1914*, Croom Helm, 1985.

Bullock, Alan, *The Life and Times of Ernest Bevin: Trade Union Leader*, Heinemann, 1960; *The Life and Times of Ernest Bevin Vol. II*, Heinemann, 1967; *Ernest Bevin: Foreign Secretary 1945–51*, Heinemann, 1983.

Burgess, K., *The Challenge of Labour*, Croom Helm, 1984.

Campbell, J., *Nye Bevan and the Mirage of British Socialism*, Weidenfeld & Nicolson, 1987.

Carlton, David, *MacDonald versus Henderson; The Foreign Policy of the Second Labour Government*, Macmillan, 1970.

Chester, H., Fay, S., and Young, H., *The Zinoviev Letter*, (Heinemann, London, 1967).

Clark, David, *Colne Valley: Radicalism to Socialism*, Longman, 1981.

Clarke, P.F., *Lancashire and the New Liberalism*, Cambridge University Press, 1971.

Cole, Margaret, *The Story of Fabian Socialism*, Heinemann, 1961.

Cowling, Maurice, *The Impact of Labour 1920–1924*, Cambridge University Press, 1971.

Cronin, J.E., *Labour and Society 1918–1979*, Batsford, 1984.

Dalton, Hugh, *Call Back Yesterday, Memoirs*, Muller, 1953.

Dalton, Hugh, *The Fateful Years, Memoirs, 1931–1945*, Muller, 1957.

Dangerfield, George, *The Strange Death of Liberal England*, Constable, 1935 and Paladin Books, 1970.

Dore, R., 'British Labour, the National government and the National interest, 1931', *Historical Studies*, September 1979.

Dowse, R.E., *Left in the Centre. The Independent Labour Party 1893–1940*, Longman, 1966.

Duffy, A.E.P., 'Differing policies and personal rivalries in the origins of the Independent Labour Party', *Victorian Studies*, vol. 6, 1962/3.

Fabian Essays (1889), Jubilee edn. Allen & Unwin, 1945.

Fleay, C., and Saunders, M., 'The Labour Spain Committee: the Labour Party Policy and the Spanish Civil War', *Historical Journal*, xxviii, 1985.

Foot, M., *Aneurin Bevan, 1887–1945*, MacGibbon & Kee, 1962; *Aneurin Bevan, 1945–1960*, Davies Poynter, 1973.

Francis, H., and Smith, D., *The Fed*, (Lawrence and Wilehart, London, 1980).

Gregory, *The Miners and British Politics, 1906–1914*, Oxford University Press, 1968.

Harris, Kenneth, *Attlee*, Weidenfeld & Nicolson, 1982.

Harrison, Martin, *Trade Unions and the Labour Party since 1945*, Allen & Unwin, 1960.

Harrison, Royden, 'The War Emergency: Workers' National Committee 1914–1920', in A. Briggs and J. Saville. eds., *Essays in Labour History*, Macmillan, 1971.

Henderson, Philip, ed., *Letters of William Morris*, Longman, 1950.

Hinton, James, *Labour and Socialism: A History of the British Labour Movement 1867–1974*, Wheatsheaf, 1983.

Hobsbawm, Eric, *Labour's Turning Point 1880–1900*, Lawrence & Wishart 1948, Harvester Press, 1974.

Hobsbawm, Eric, *Labouring Man*, Weidenfeld & Nicolson, 1968.

Howard, C., 'Expectation born to death: the local Labour Party expansion in the 1920s', in J. Winter, ed., *The Working Class in Modern British History: Essays in Honour of Henry Pelling*, Cambridge Univerisity Press, 1983.

Howell, David, *British Workers and the Independent Labour Party 1888–1906*, Manchester University Press, 1983.

Jones, T., *Whitehall Diary Vol. I*, ed., K. Middlemass, Oxford University Press, 1969.

Kent, W., *John Burns. Labour's lost leader*, Williams & Norgate, 1950.

Labour Party, *Among Our Souvenirs*, (London, 1975).

Laybourn, Keith and Reynolds, Jack, *Liberalism and the Rise of Labour 1890–1918*, Croom Helm, 1984.

Laybourn, Keith, *Philip Snowden*, Gower/Wildwood, 1988.

Laybourn, Keith, *The Rise of Labour: The Labour Party c. 1890–1979*, Edward Arnold, 1988.

Lyman, R.W., *The First Labour Government 1924*, Chapman & Hill, 1957.

Lyman, R.W., 'James Ramsay MacDonald and the leadership of the Labour Party 1918–1922', *Journal of British Studies*, vol. 2, 1962/3.

Lyman, R.W., 'The British Labour Party: the conflict between Socialist ideals and practical policies between the wars', *Journal of British Studies*, vol. 5, 1965/6.

MacNeill Weir, L., *The Tragedy of Ramsay MacDonald*, Secker & Warburg, 1938.

Marquand, David, *Ramsay MacDonald*, Jonathan Cape, 1977.

McKibbin, R.I., *The Evolution of the Labour Party 1910–1924*, Oxford University Press, 1974.

McKibbin, R.I., 'James Ramsay MacDonald and the problems of the independence of the Labour Party, 1910–1914', *Journal of Modern History*, vol. 42, 1970.

Middlemass, R.K., *The Clydesiders*, Hutchinson, 1965.

Miliband, Ralph, *Parliamentary Socialism*, Merlin, 1972 edition.

Morgan, K.O., 'The New Liberalism and the Challenge of Labour: The Welsh Experience 1885–1929', in K.D. Brown, ed., *Essays in Anti-Labour History*, 1974.

Morgan, K.O., *Labour in Power 1945–1951*, Clarendon Press, 1984.

Mowat, C.L., 'Ramsay MacDonald and the Labour Party', in A. Briggs and J. Saville, eds., *Essays in Labour History*, Macmillan, 1971.

Naylor, J.F., *Labour's International Policy. The Labour Party in the 1930's*, Weidenfeld & Nicolson, 1969.

Pease, E.R., *The History of the Fabian Society*, (1916, 1963).

Pelling, Henry, *The Origins of the Labour Party 1880–1900*, Macmillan, 1954.

Pelling, Henry, *A Short History of the Labour Party*, Macmillan, 3rd edition, 1968.

Pelling, Henry, *Popular Politics and Society in late Victorian Britain*, Macmillan, 1968.

Pimlott, Ben., *Labour and the Left in the 1930s*, Cambridge University Press, 1977.

Pimlott, Ben., *Hugh Dalton*, Jonathan Cape, 1985.

Pimlott, Ben., ed., *The Second World War Diary of Hugh Dalton 1940–45*, Jonathan Cape, 1986.

Pimlott, Ben., ed., *The Political Diary of Hugh Dalton, 1918–1940 and 1945–1960*, Jonathan Cape, 1987.

Poirier, Philip P., *The Advent of the Labour Party*, Allen & Unwin, 1958.

Price, Richard, *Labour in British Society*, Croom Helm, 1986.

Purdue, A.W., 'The Liberals and the Labour Party in North East Politics', *International Review of Social History*, xxvi, 1981.

Reynolds, Jack and Laybourn, Keith, 'The Emergence of the Independent Labour Party in Bradford', *International Review of Social*, xx, 1975.

Reynolds, Jack and Laybourn, Keith, *Labour Heartland*, Bradford University Press, 1987.

Skidelsky, R., *Politicians and the Slump: The Labour Government of 1929–1931*, Macmillan, 1967.

Stevenson, J., and Cook, C., *The Slump*, (Jonathan Cape, London, 1977).

Thompson, E.P., 'Homage to Tom Maguire', in A. Briggs and J. Saville, eds., *Essays in Labour History*, Macmillan, 1960.

Thompson, E.P., *William Morris: Romantic to Revolutionary*, Merlin, 1977 ed.

Thompson, Paul, *Socialists, Liberals and Labour: The Struggle for London 1885–1914*, Routledge & Kegan Paul, 1967.

Thompson, W., *Victor Grayson MP*, (Worker Press, Huddersfield, 1910).

Tittman, H.H., *James Ramsay MacDonald*, (1929).

Torr, Dona, *Tom Mann and his Times*, vol. 1, 1856–1890, Lawrence and Wishart, 1956.

Trevelyan, C.P., Labour Party Conference, *Annual Report 1936*, Labour Party, 1936.

Tsuzuki, C., *H.M. Hyndman and British Socialism*, Oxford University Press, 1961.

Watkins, K.W., *Britain Divided*, Nelson, 1963.

Weir, L. MacNeill, *The Tragedy of Ramsay MacDonald*, Secker & Warburg, 1938.

Williams, P.M., *Hugh Gaitskell*, Oxford University Press, 1982.

Williams, P.M., ed., *The Diary of Hugh Gaitskell*, Jonathan Cape, 1983.

Wilson, Trevor, *The Downfall of the Liberal Party 1914–1935*, Collins, 1966.

Winter, J.M., *Socialism and the Challenge of War: Ideas and Politics in Britain, 1912–1918*, Routledge & Kegan Paul, 1974.

APPENDIX:
THE LABOUR VOTE 1900–1951

General Elections	Votes	MPs elected	% share of total vote
1900	63,304	2	1.8
1906	329,748	30	5.9
1910 (Jan.)	505,657	40	7.6
1910 (Dec.)	371,772	42	7.1
1918	2,385,472	63	22.2
1922	4,241,383	142	29.5
1923	4,438,508	191	30.5
1924	5,489,077	151	33.0
1929	8,389,512	288	37.1
1931	6,649,630	52	30.6
1935	8,325,491	154	37.9
1945	11,995,491	393	47.8
1950	13,266,176	315	46.1
1951	13,948,883	295	48.8

ACKNOWLEDGEMENTS

The list of those to whom I must express thanks is lengthy. The librarians and archivists of West Yorkshire have given generously of their time and knowledge and, though I cannot mention every name, I must express my thanks to Elvira Wilmott, David James and Dr Alan Betteridge, and their staffs.

Although financial help was limited I did receive some research funds from Professor Burnip, Dean of Research of Huddersfield Polytechnic, without which it would have been difficult to visit the Public Record Office, Kew, London and the Labour Party Archives, at Walworth Road, London.

My colleagues at Huddersfield Polytechnic were more than helpful (especially Dr David Wright), as were many other historians who live and work in West Yorkshire. But I must, above all, thank Jack Reynolds, who first revealed the existence of the Independent Labour Party to me nearly a quarter of a century ago when, as a student, I took his special subject course. Since then he has remained a seminal force in my education and research.

I would also like to thank Stephen Bird, the Labour Party's Archivist, for permission to quote from the records of the Labour Party. Crown copyright material in the the Public Record Office is reproduced by permission of the Controller of Her Majesty's Stationery Office. James Ramsay MacDonald's Diaries were, in his own words, 'meant as notes to guide and revive memory as regards happenings and must on no account be published as they are'. In accordance with his request, and the approval of the heirs of Malcolm MacDonald, only selected extracts of MacDonald's work have been included. The author and the publisher also wish to apologise for any inadvertent infringement of copyright and have sought to keep within the publishers convention in the use of some recently published secondary sources.
